PIANO · VOCAL · GUITAR

THE BEST LOVE SONGS EVER

ISBN 0-7935-1004-X

Hal Leonard Publishing Corporation

7777 West Bluemound Road P.O. Box 13819 Milwaukee, WI 53213

CONTENTS

THE BEST LOVE SONGS EVER

AND I LOVE HER

Words and Music by JOHN LENNON
and PAUL McCARTNEY

I give her all my love, that's all I do.
She gives me ev-'ry-thing and ten-der-ly.
Bright are the stars that shine, dark is the sky.

And if you saw my love you'd love her too.
The kiss my lov-er brings she brings to me.
I know this love of mine will nev-er die.

I love And I love And I love

I know this love of mine___ will nev-er die.___

And I love___ her.___

___ her.___

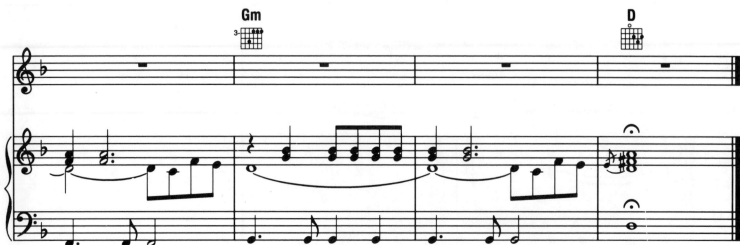

AND I LOVE YOU SO

Words and Music by
DON McLEAN

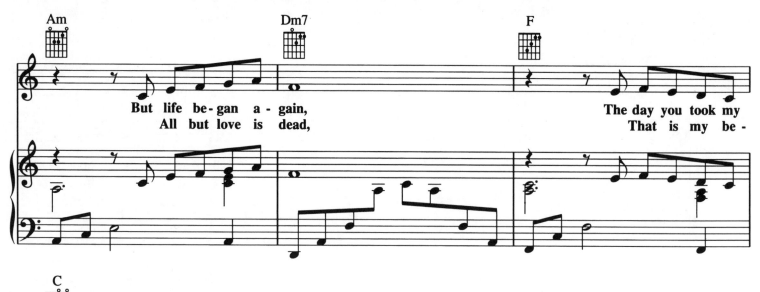

But life be-gan a-gain,
All but love is dead,
The day you took my
That is my be-

hand. _____
lief. _____
And, yes, I know how

lone-ly life can be, _____
(love-less)
The shad-ows fol-low me and the

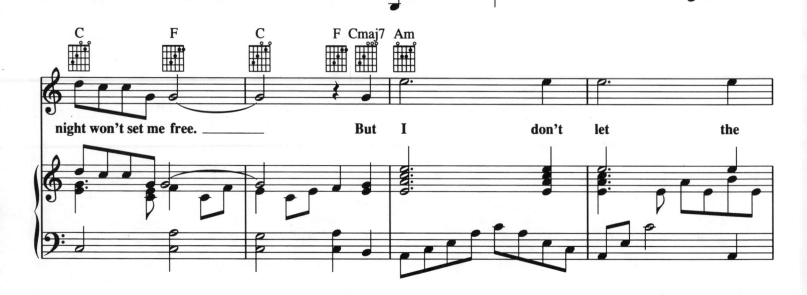

night won't set me free. _____
But I don't let the

ANNIVERSARY SONG

By AL JOLSON
and SAUL CHAPLIN

Moderately Slow

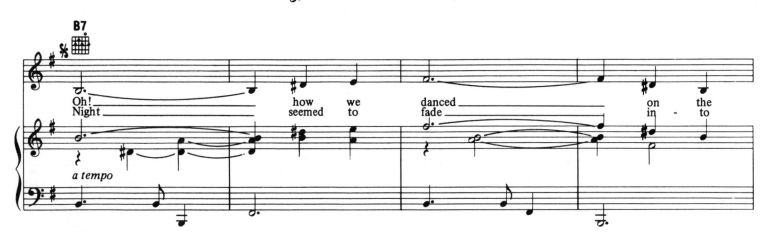

Oh! _____ how we danced _____ on the
Night _____ seemed to fade _____ in to

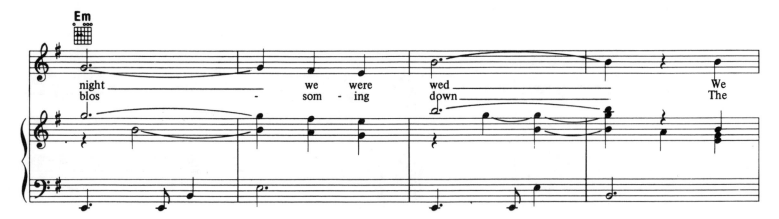

night _____ we were wed _____ We
blos - som - ing down _____ The

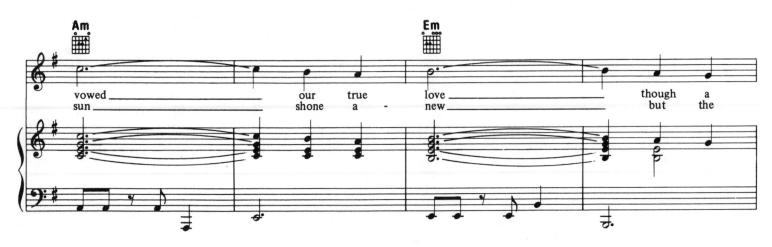

vowed _____ our true love _____ though a
sun _____ shone a - new _____ but the

CAN'T HELP FALLING IN LOVE

Words and Music by
GEORGE DAVID WEISS, HUGO PERETTI,
and LUIGI CREATORE

Moderately Slow

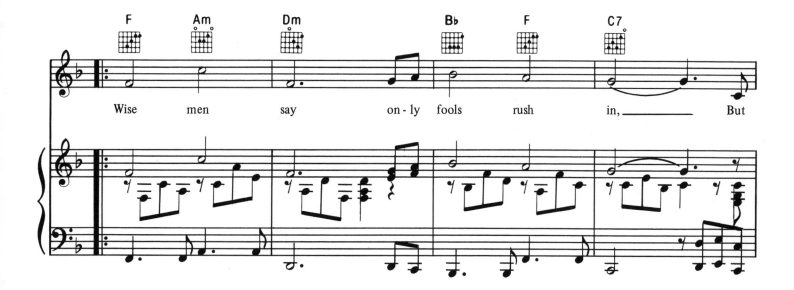

Wise men say on-ly fools rush in, _____ But

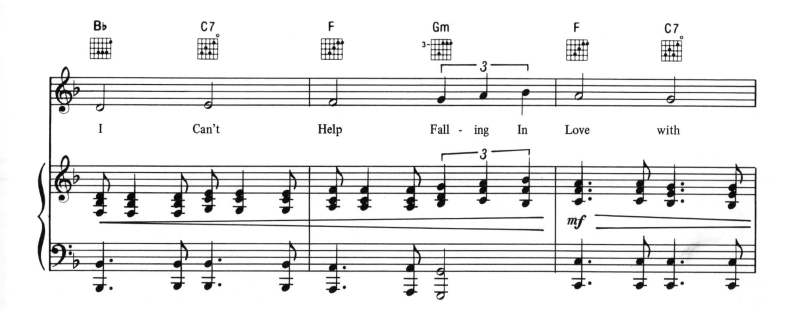

I Can't Help Fall-ing In Love with

BECAUSE I LOVE YOU
(THE POSTMAN'S SONG)

Words and Music by
WARREN ALLEN BROOKS

1. I got your let-ter from the post-
2.,3. If you should feel that

man just the oth-er day
I don't real-ly care
so I de-cid-ed to write you this song
and that you're start-ing to lose ground.

to be your light, ___ to be ___ your guide. ___

Repeat and Fade

CAN'T SMILE WITHOUT YOU

Moderately, with a relaxed beat

Words and Music by CHRIS ARNOLD,
DAVID MARTIN and GEOFF MORROW

You know, I

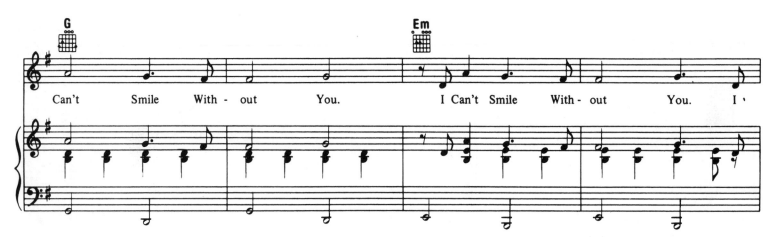

Can't Smile With-out You. I Can't Smile With-out You. I

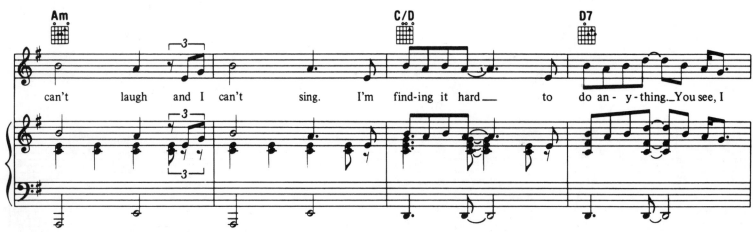

can't laugh and I can't sing. I'm find-ing it hard____ to do an-y-thing. You see, I

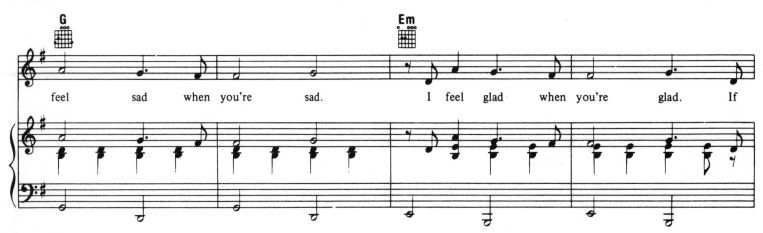

feel sad when you're sad. I feel glad when you're glad. If

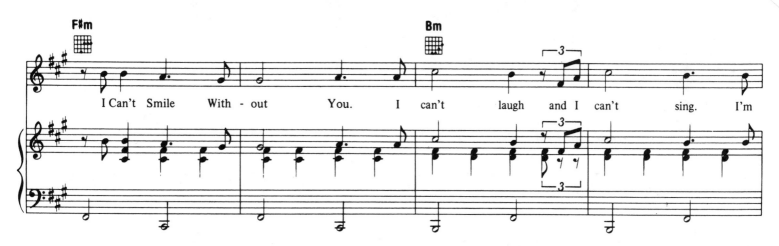

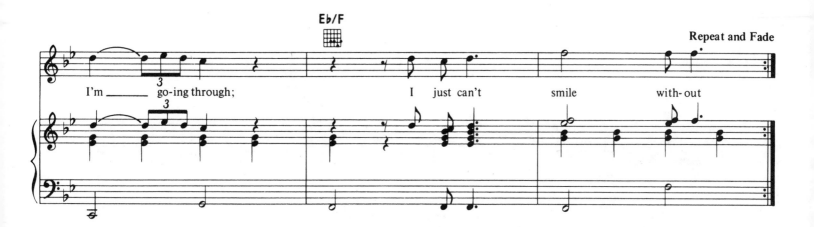

CANDLE ON THE WATER

Words and Music by
AL KASHA and JOEL HIRSCHHORN

Romantic, Spiritual Ballad (♩= 66)

I'll be your can-dle on the wa-ter,
My love for you will al-ways
'Til ev-'ry wave is warm and

I'll be your can-dle on the wa-ter,

burn.
bright.
I know you're lost and drift-ing.
My soul is there be-side you.
But the clouds are lift-ing,
Let this can-dle guide you

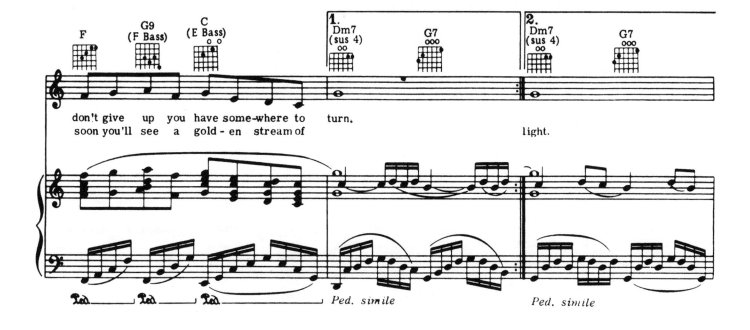

don't give up you have some-where to turn.
soon you'll see a gold-en stream of light.

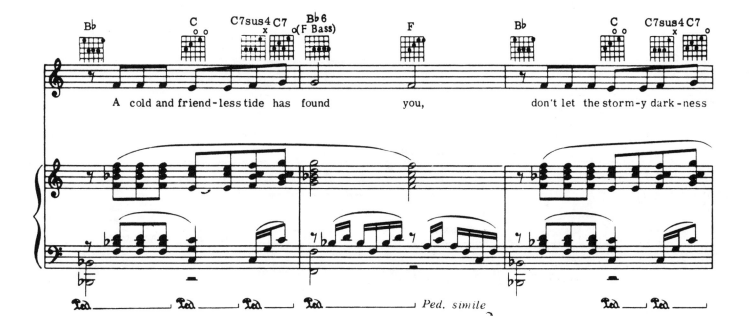

A cold and friend-less tide has found you, don't let the storm-y dark-ness

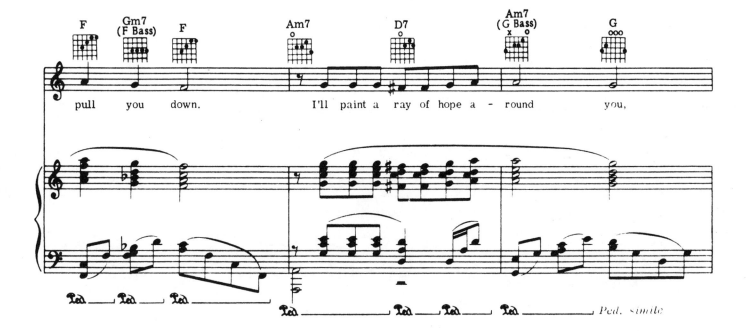

pull you down. I'll paint a ray of hope a - round you,

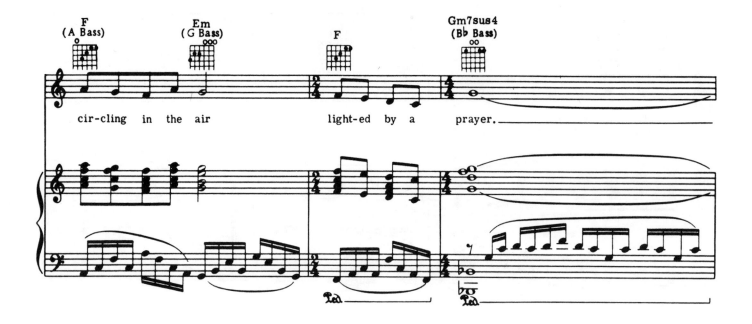

cir-cling in the air light-ed by a prayer.

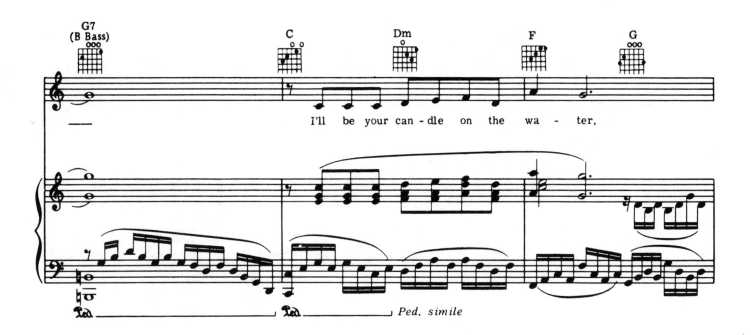

I'll be your can-dle on the wa-ter, this flame in-side of me will grow.

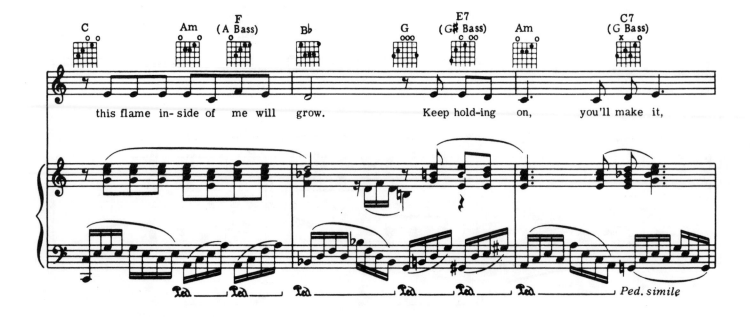

this flame in-side of me will grow. Keep hold-ing on, you'll make it,

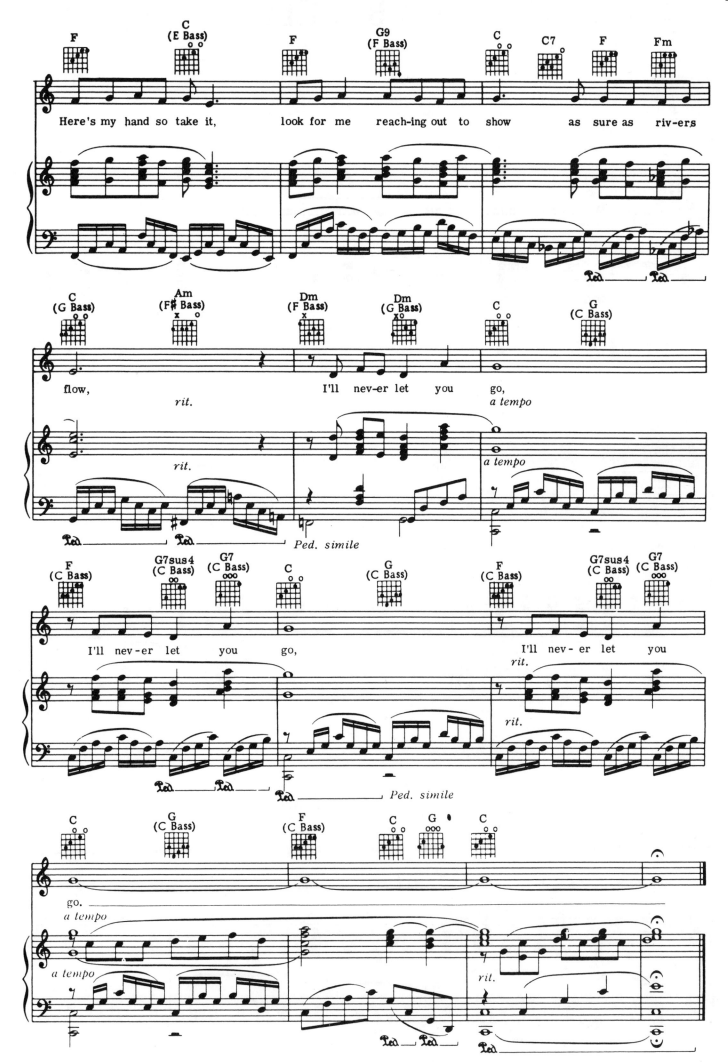

(THEY LONG TO BE) CLOSE TO YOU

Lyric by HAL DAVID
Music by BURT BACHARACH

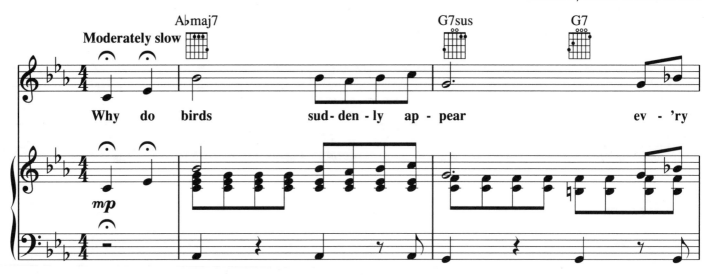

Why do birds sud-den-ly ap-pear ev-'ry

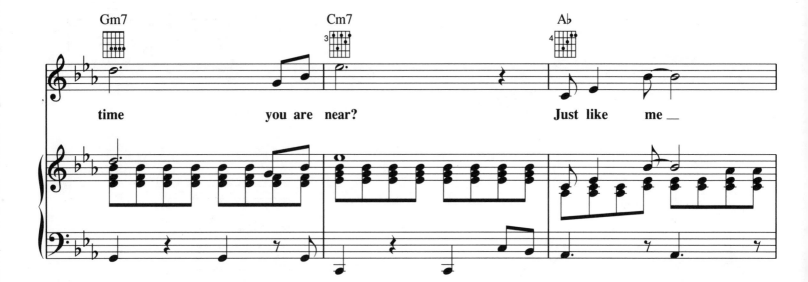

time you are near? Just like me

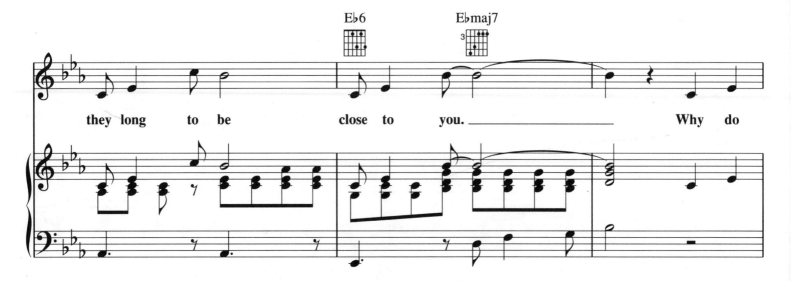

they long to be close to you. _____ Why do

an - gels got to - geth - er and de - cid - ed to cre - ate a dream come

true. So, they sprink - led moon dust in your hair of

gold and star - light in your eyes of blue. That is

why all the {boys} {girls} in town fol - low

COULD I HAVE THIS DANCE

Words and Music by WAYLAND HOLYFIELD
and BOB HOUSE

Moderately

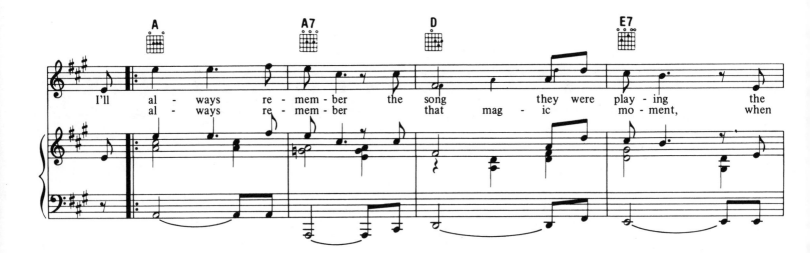

I'll al - ways re - mem - ber the song they were play - ing the
al - ways re - mem - ber that mag - ic mo - ment, when

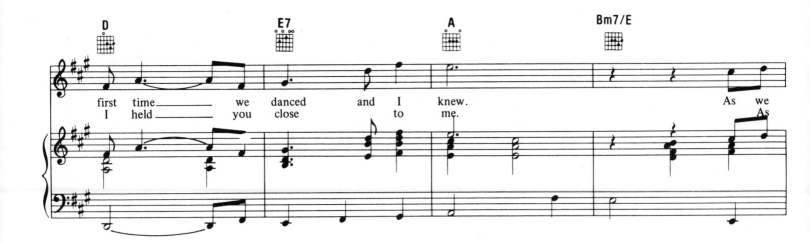

first time ___ we danced and I knew. As we
I held ___ you close to me. As

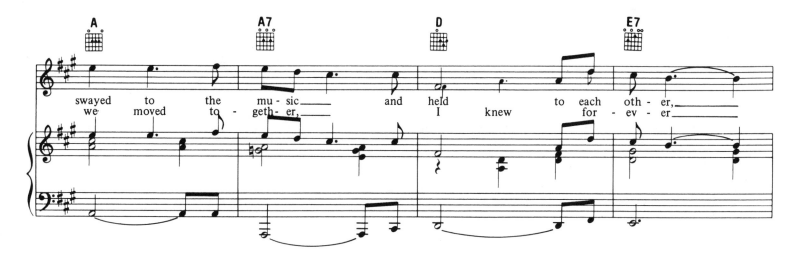

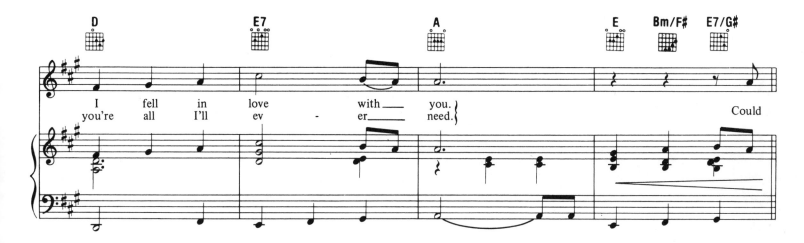

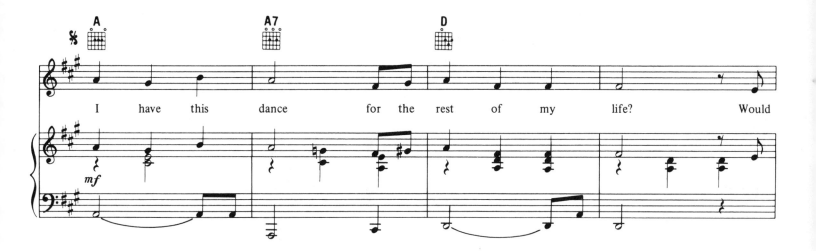

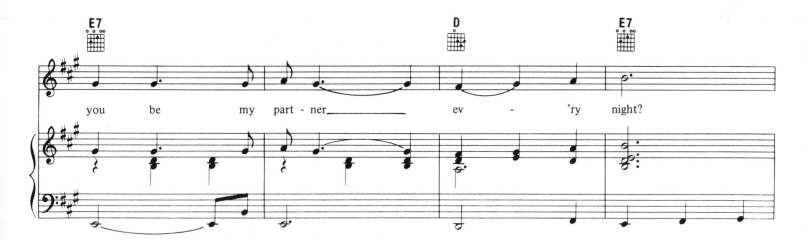

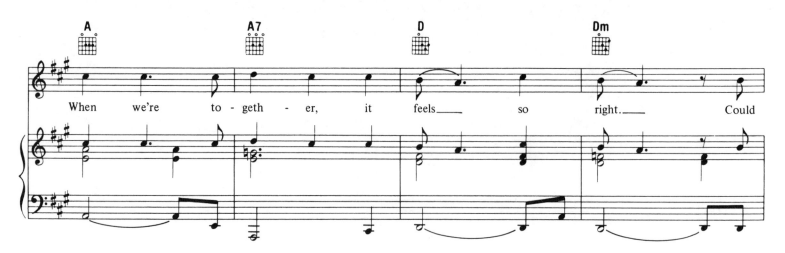

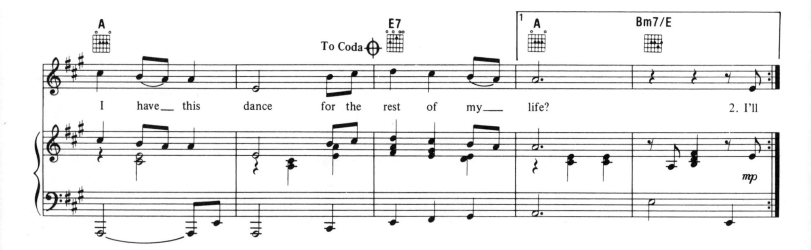

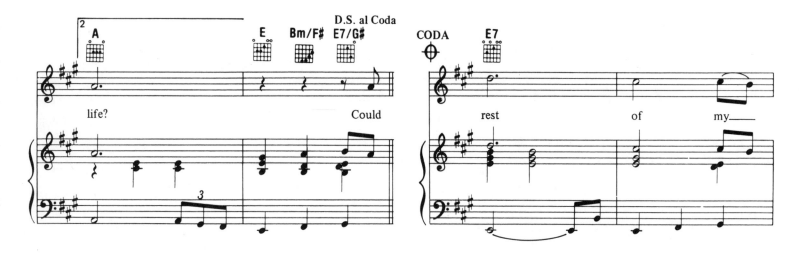

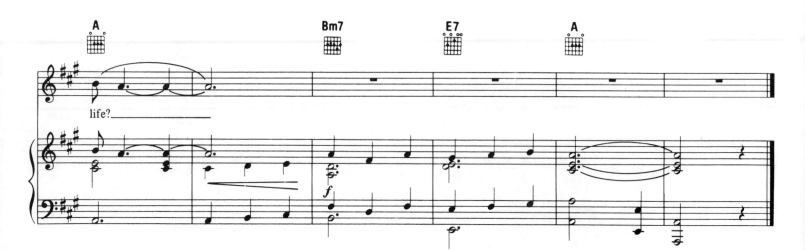

FALLING IN LOVE WITH LOVE
(From "THE BOYS FROM SYRACUSE")

Words by LORENZ HART
Music by RICHARD RODGERS

Moderate Waltz

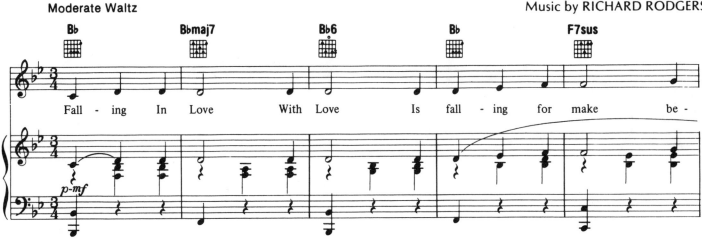

Fall - ing In Love With Love Is fall - ing for make be -

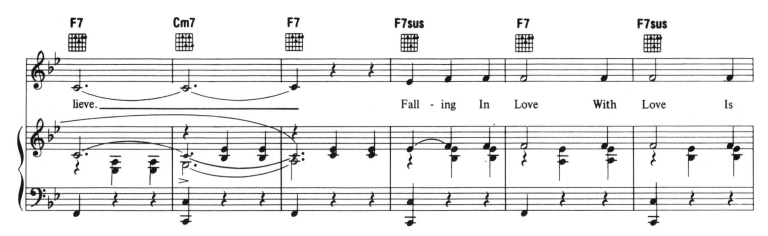

lieve. _____ Fall - ing In Love With Love Is

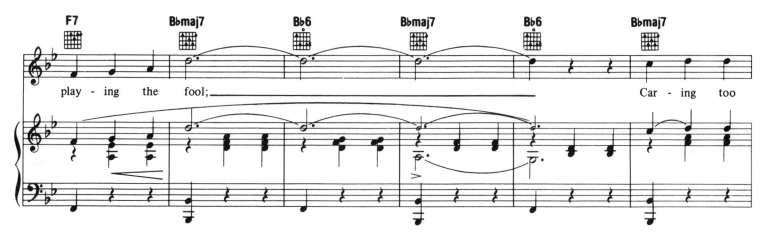

play - ing the fool; _____ Car - ing too

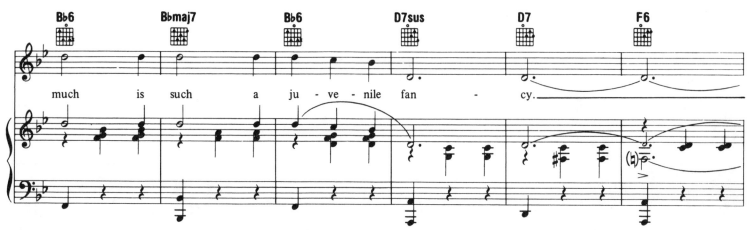

much is such a ju - ve - nile fan - cy. _____

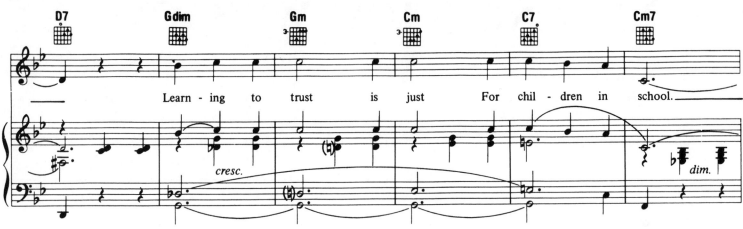

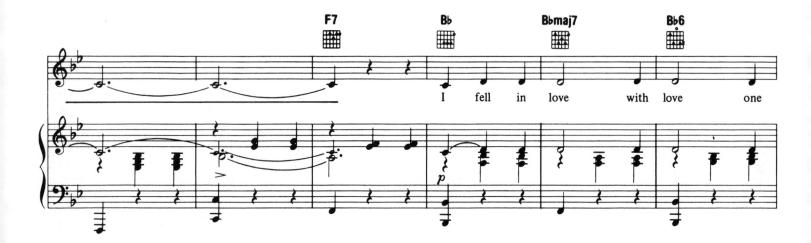

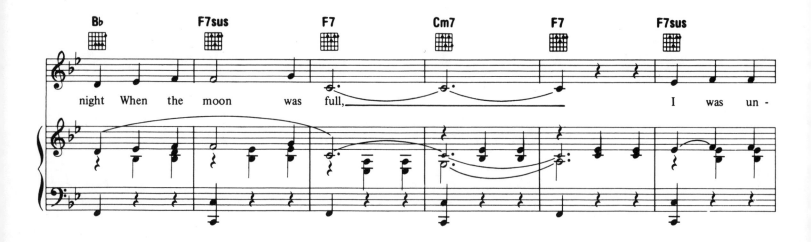

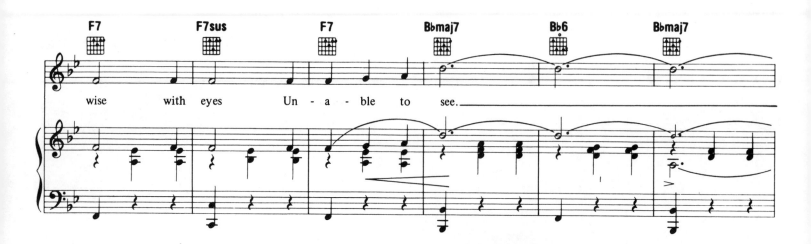

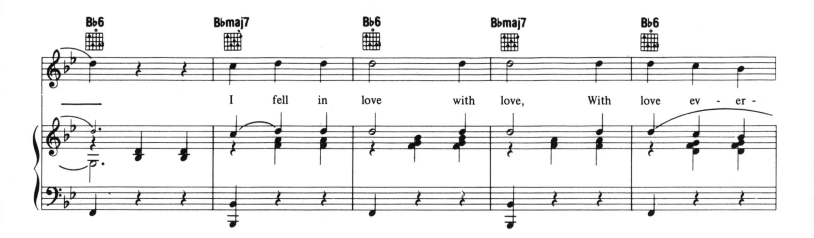

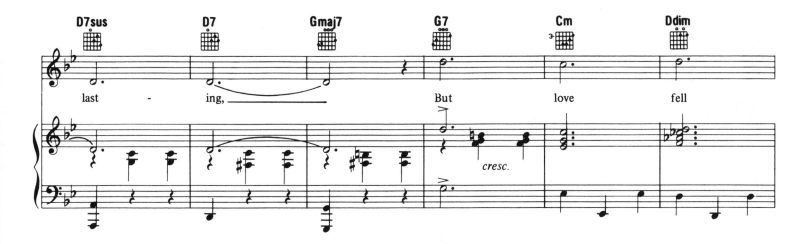

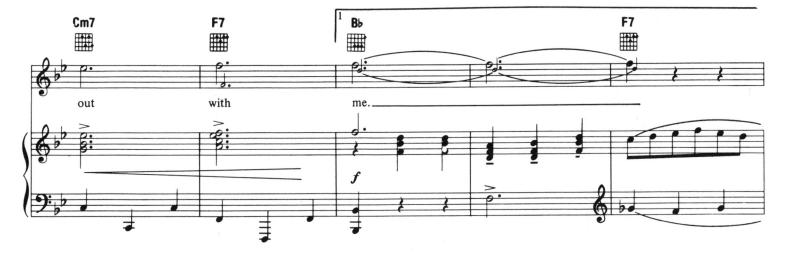

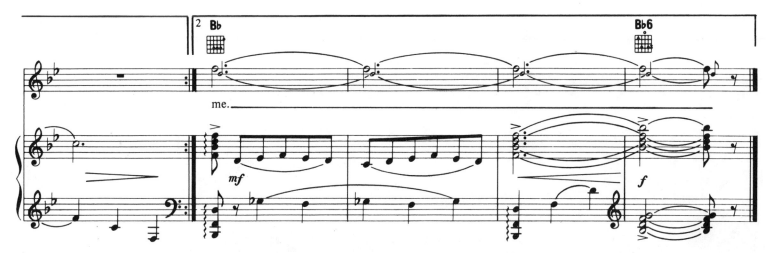

DARLING, JE VOUS AIME BEAUCOUP

Words and Music by
ANNA SOSENKO

DON'T KNOW MUCH

Words and Music by BARRY MANN,
CYNTHIA WEIL and TOM SNOW

ENDLESS LOVE

Words and Music by
LIONEL RICHIE

Moderately Slow

My love ___
Two hearts ___

There's on - ly you in my life ___
Two hearts that you beat as ___ one ___

The on - ly thing that's right ___
Our lives have just be - gun ___

For -

My first ___ love ___
ev - er ___

You're ev - 'ry breath ___ that I take ___
I hold you close ___ in my arms

FEELINGS
(¿DIME?)

English Words and Music by MORRIS ALBERT
Spanish Lyric by THOMAS FUNDORA

Moderately Slow

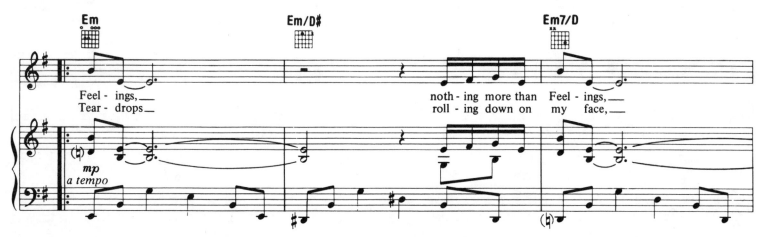

Feel - ings,___ nothing more than Feel - ings,
Tear - drops___ roll - ing down on my face,

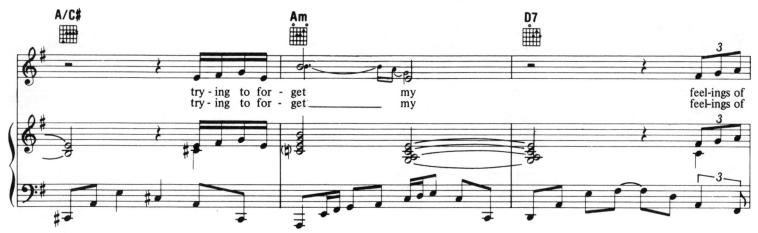

try - ing to for - get my
try - ing to for - get___ my

feel-ings of
feel-ings of

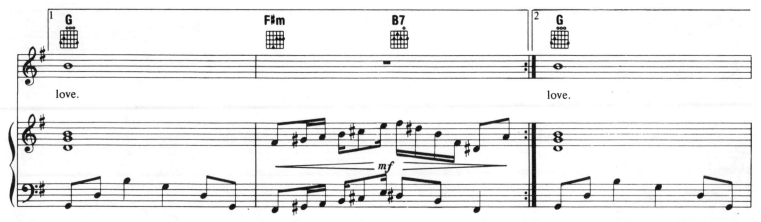

love.

love.

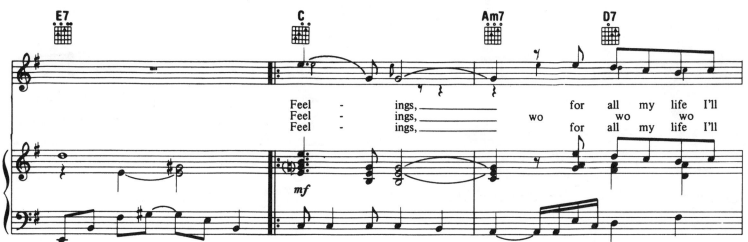

Feel - ings, _____ for all my life I'll
Feel - ings, _____ wo wo wo for all my life I'll

feel - it. I wish I'd nev - er met _____ you, girl;
Feel - ings. Wo wo wo feel _____ you
feel - it. I wish I'd nev - er met _____ you, girl;

you'll nev - er come a - gain.
a - gain in my
you'll nev - er come a -

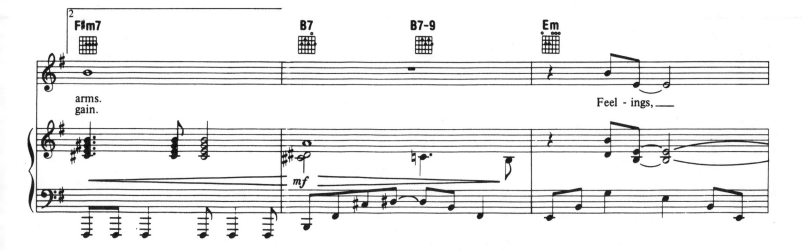

arms.
gain.
Feel - ings, ___

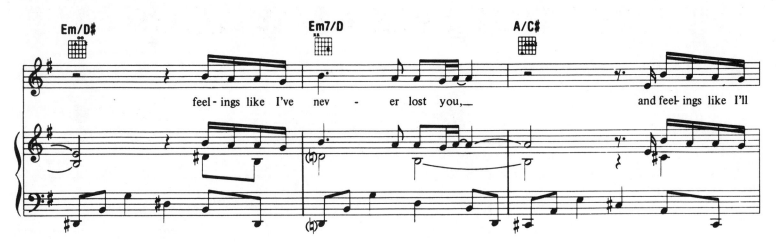

feel-ings like I've nev - er lost you,___ and feel-ings like I'll

nev - er have you___ a - gain in my {heart. life.}

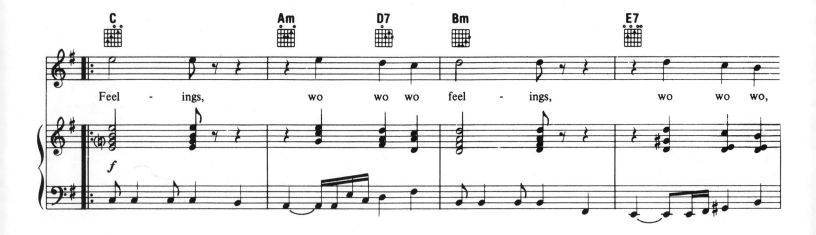

Feel - ings, wo wo wo feel-ings, wo wo wo,

Repeat and Fade

Feel - ings a - gain in my arms.

THE FIRST TIME EVER I SAW YOUR FACE

Words and Music by
EWAN MacCOLL

FOR ALL WE KNOW

(From the Motion Picture "LOVERS AND OTHER STRANGERS")

Words by ROBB WILSON and JAMES GRIFFIN
Music by FRED KARLIN

Moderato, with a light beat

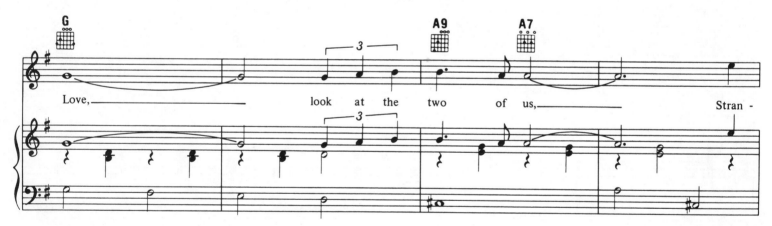

Love, _____ look at the two of us, _____ Stran-

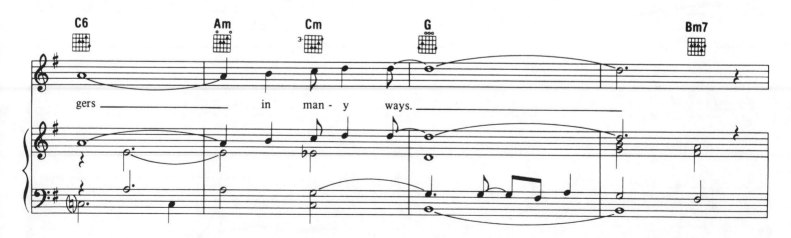

gers _____ in man-y ways. _____

FOREVER AND EVER, AMEN

Words and Music by DON SCHLITZ
and PAUL OVERSTREET

MCA music publishing

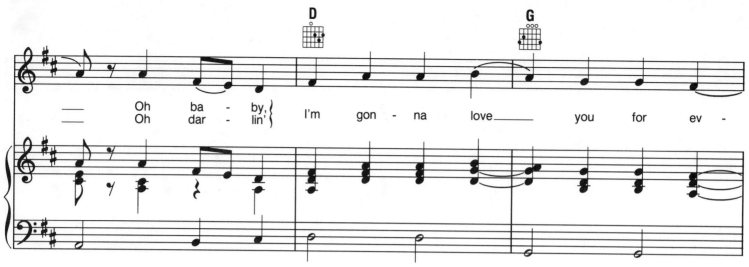

Oh ba - by;
Oh dar - lin' } I'm gon - na love_____ you for ev -

- er,_____ for - ev - er and ev -

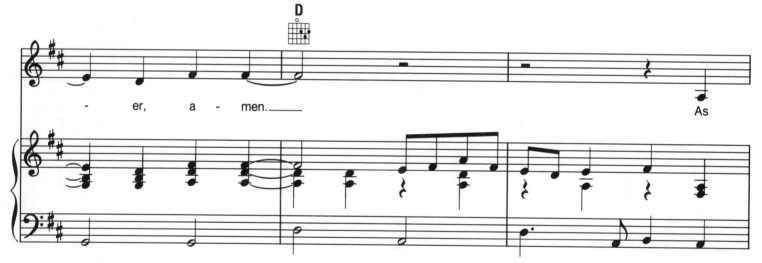

- er, a - men._____ As

long as old men_____ sit and talk a - bout_____ the wea -

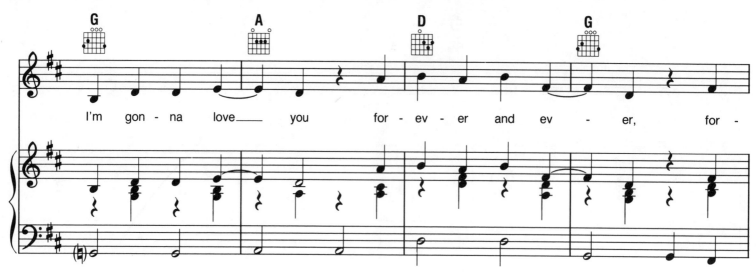

I'm gon-na love____ you for- ev- er and ev- er, for-

ev- er and ev- er, a - men.

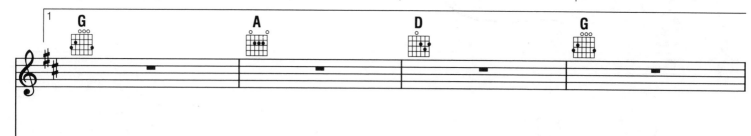

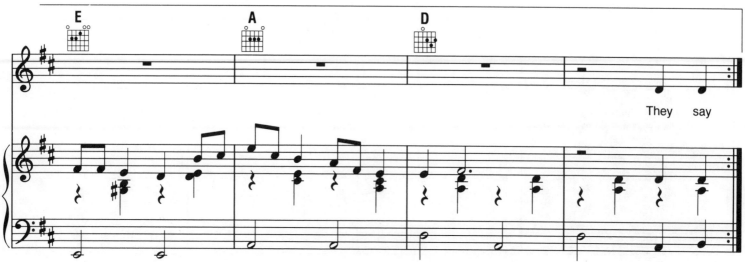

They say

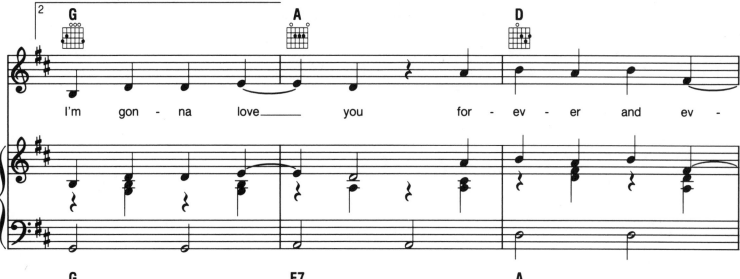

I'm gon - na love____ you for - ev - er and ev -

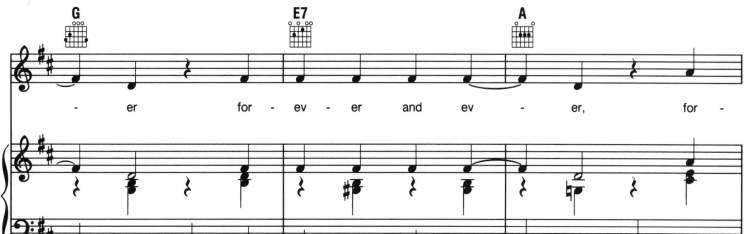

- er for - ev - er and ev - er, for -

ev - er and ev - er, for - ev - er and ev -

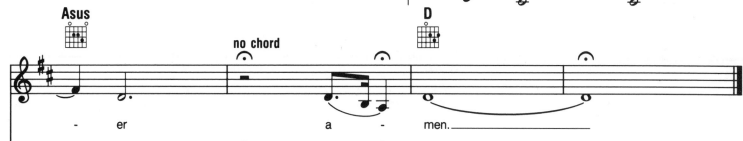

- er a - men.____

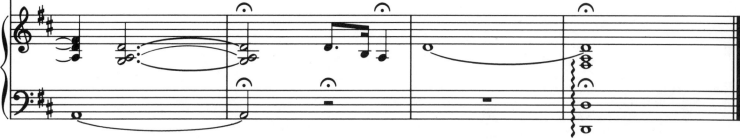

HERE AND NOW

Words and Music by TERRY STEELE
and DAVID ELLIOT

D.S. al Coda

glad to take ___ the vow. Here and ___ now, _____ oh, ___ I

Your love is all ___ I, { need. *Vocal ad lib.* ___ yeah, _____

yeah. _____ Uh, yeah. _____ Ay ah, ___ love is all ___ I

last time rit.

Yeah. _____

HOW DEEP IS YOUR LOVE

Words and Music by BARRY GIBB,
ROBIN GIBB and MAURICE GIBB

Moderately

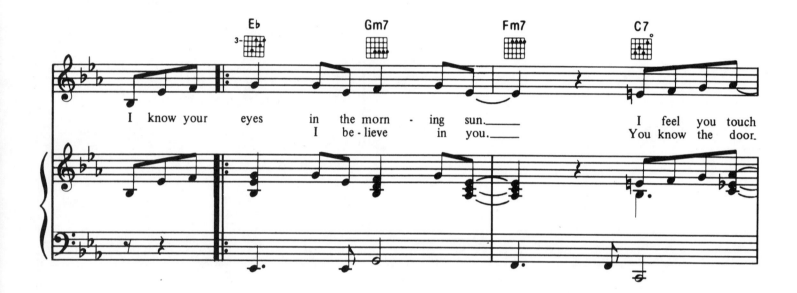

I know your eyes in the morn-ing sun.___ I feel you touch
I be-lieve in you.___ You know the door.

___ me in the pour-ing rain.___ And the mo-ment that you wan-der far___
___ to my ver-y soul.___ You're the light ___ in my deep-est, dark

I.O.U.

Words and Music by
AUSTIN ROBERTS & KERRY CHATER

Moderately Slow Ballad

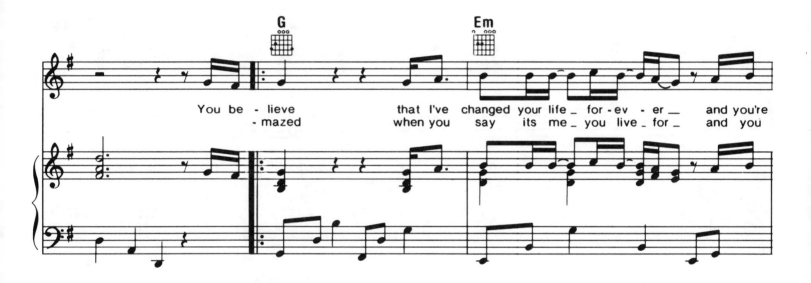

You be-lieve that I've changed your life _ for-ev-er _ and you're
-mazed when you say its me _ you live _ for _ and you

nev-er gon-na find _ an-oth-er some-bod-y like me. _ And you
know that when _ I'm hold-ing, you you're right where you be-long. _ And my

I JUST FALL IN LOVE AGAIN

Words and Music by
LARRY HERBSTRITT, STEPHEN H. DORFF,
GLORIA SKLEROV and HARRY LLOYD

I LOVE YOU

Words and Music by
COLE PORTER

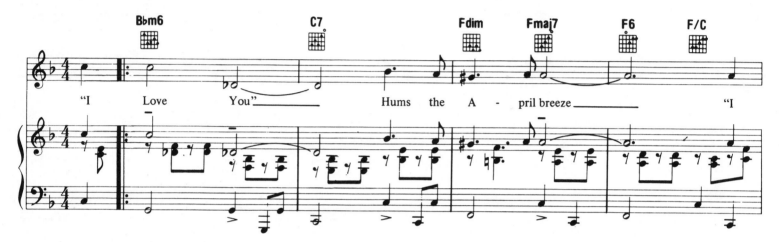

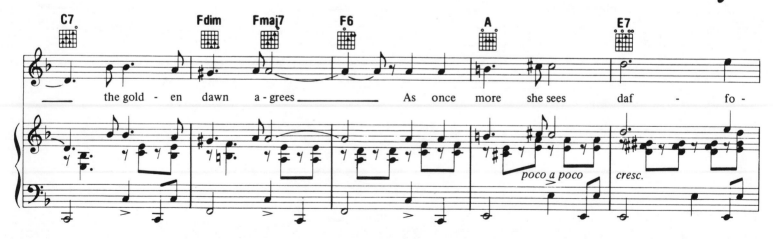

I LOVE YOU TRULY

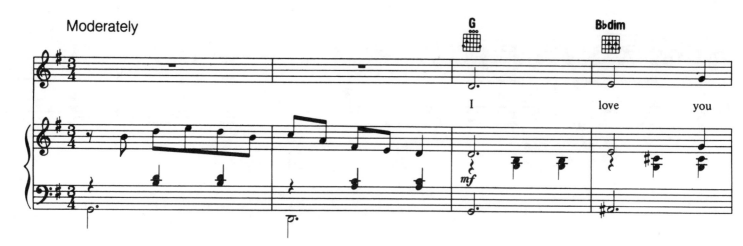

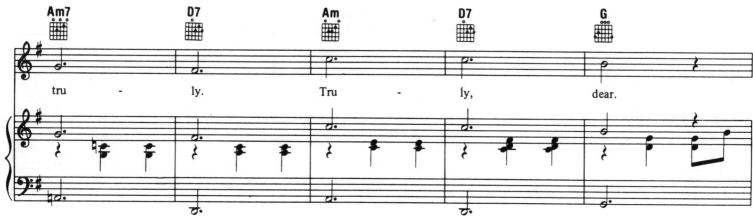

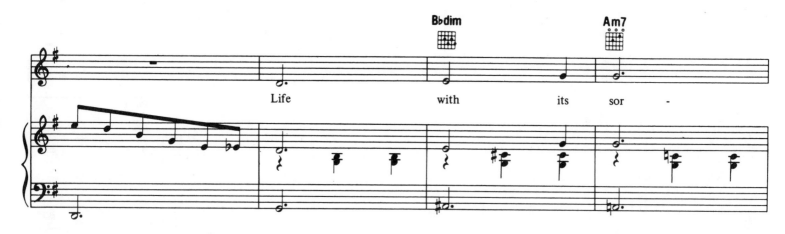

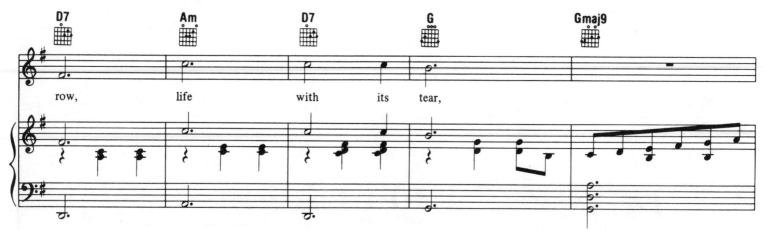

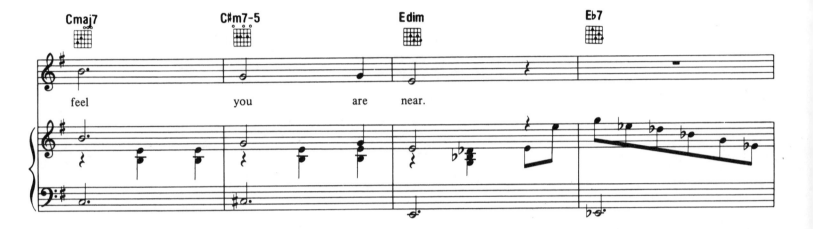

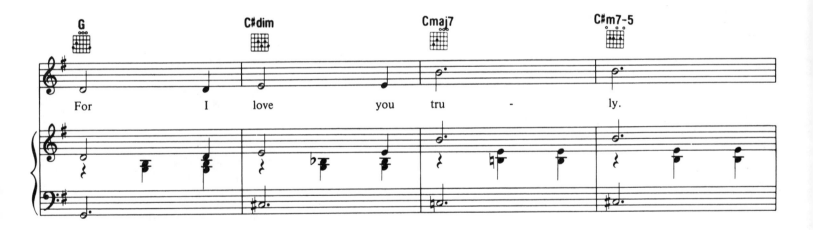

I WANT YOU, I NEED YOU, I LOVE YOU

Words by MAURICE MYSELS
Music by IRA KOSLOFF

Moderately Slow

Hold me close, __ hold me tight; __ make me thrill __ with de-light. __ Let me know __ where I stand __ from the

start. __ I Want You, I Need You, I Love You __ with all my

heart. Ev-'ry time __ that you're near __ all my cares __ dis-ap-pear. __ Dar-ling,

IF WE ONLY HAVE LOVE

English lyrics by
MORT SHUMAN and ERIC BLAU
Original French lyrics by JACQUES BREL
Music by JACQUES BREL

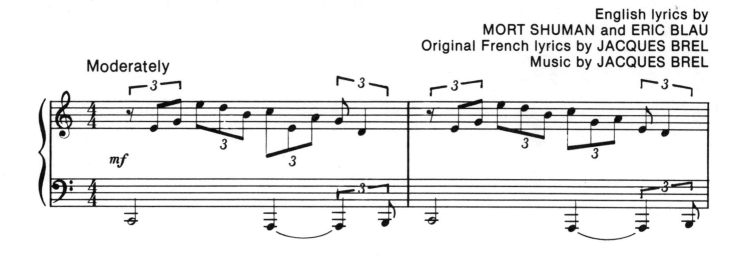

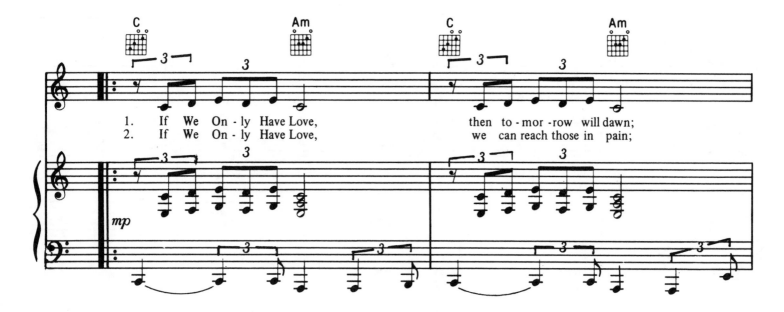

1. If We On-ly Have Love, then to-mor-row will dawn;
2. If We On-ly Have Love, we can reach those in pain;

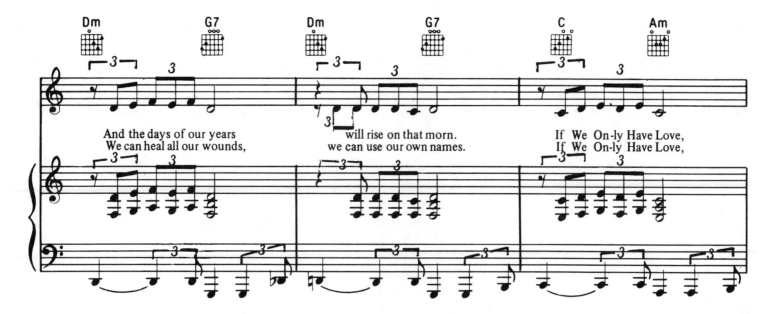

And the days of our years will rise on that morn. If We On-ly Have Love,
We can heal all our wounds, we can use our own names. If We On-ly Have Love,

IF YOU REMEMBER ME

Words by CAROLE BAYER SAGER
Music by MARVIN HAMLISCH

Moderately slow

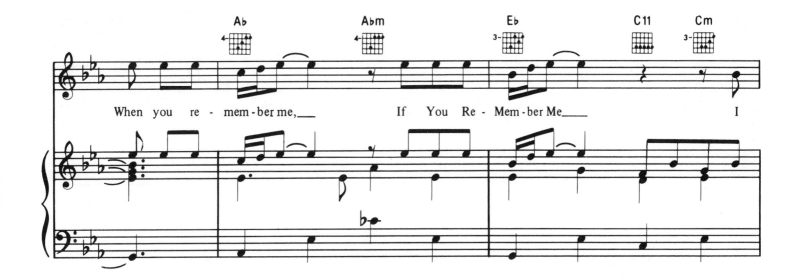

When you re-mem-ber me,___ If You Re-Mem-ber Me___ I

hope you see it's not the way I want it to be.___ Oh, I'd be with you now,___ but where-

JUST THE WAY YOU ARE

Words and Music by
BILLY JOEL

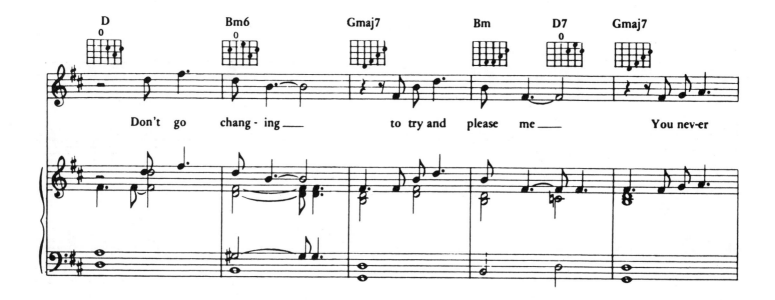

Don't go chang-ing ____ to try and please me ____ You nev-er

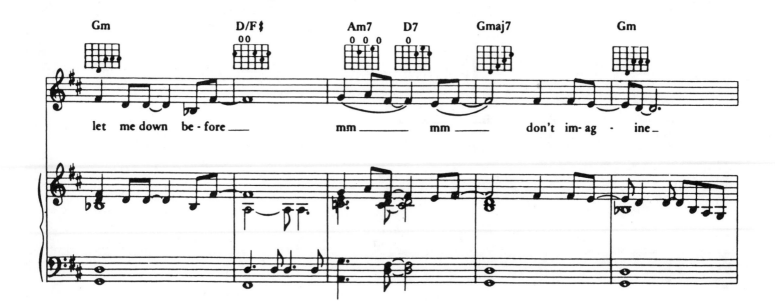

let me down be-fore ____ mm ____ mm ____ don't im-ag - ine ____

LONGER

Words and Music by
DAN FOGELBERG

Moderate Ballad

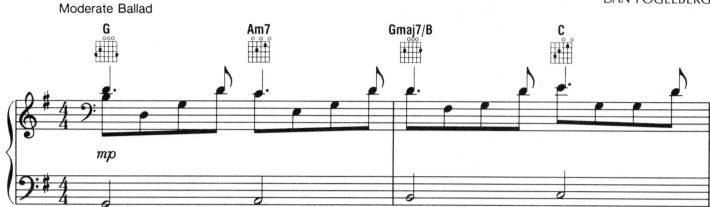

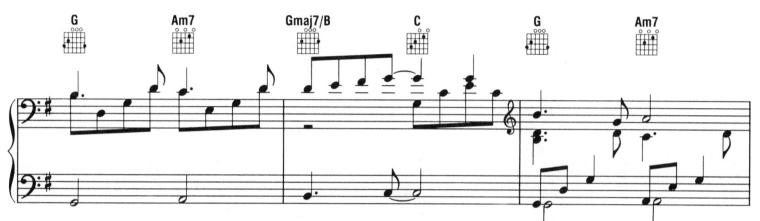

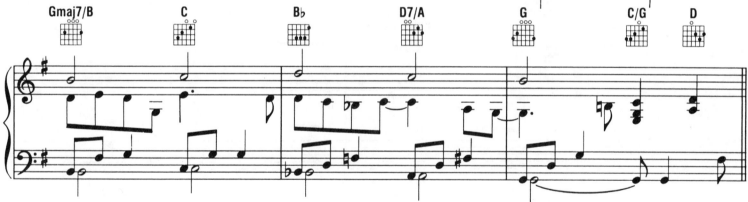

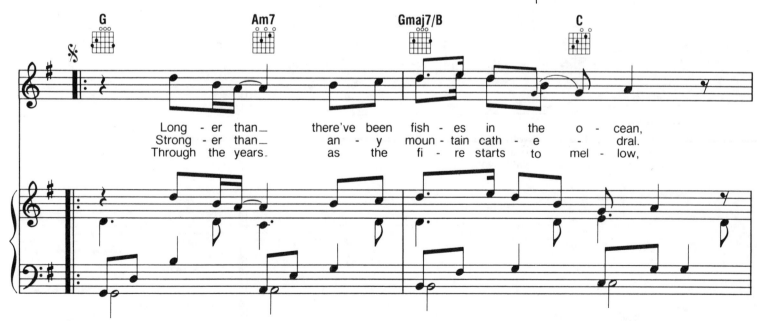

Long - er than_ there've been fish - es in the o - cean,
Strong - er than_ an - y moun - tain cath - e - dral.
Through the years_ as the fi - re starts to mel - low,

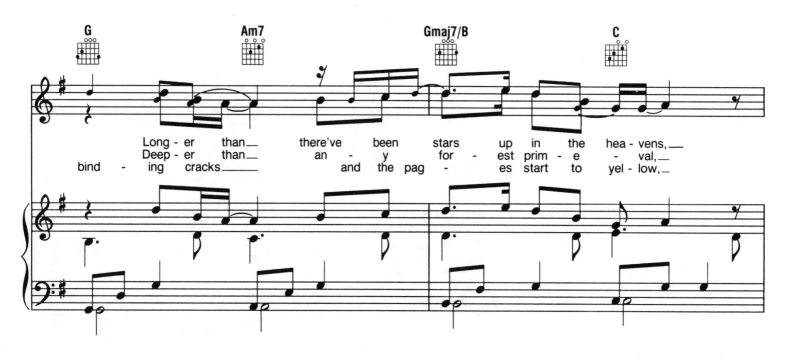

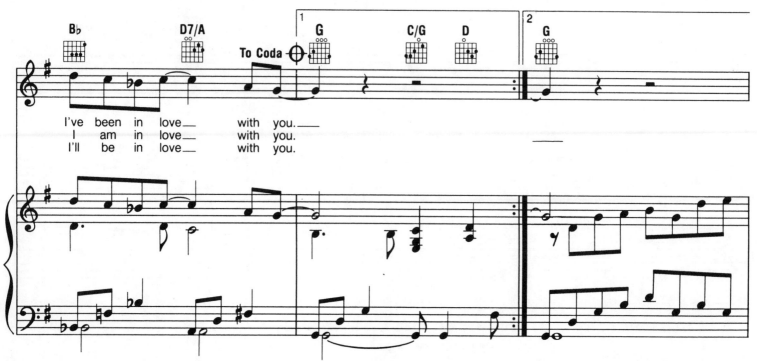

THE LAST TIME I FELT LIKE THIS

(From the Universal Picture "Same Time, Next Year")

Words by ALAN BERGMAN
and MARILYN BERGMAN
Music by MARVIN HAMLISCH

Slow Ballad tempo

Hel - lo, I don't_ e - ven know_ your name, but I'm hop-in' all__ the
lo, I can't_ wait till we're_ a - lone, some - where qui - et on__ our

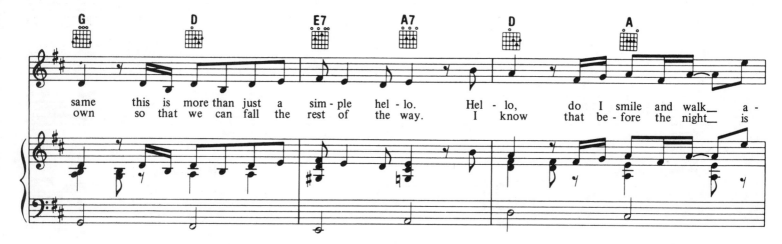

same this is more than just a sim - ple hel - lo. Hel - lo, do I smile and walk__ a -
own so that we can fall the rest of the way. I know that be - fore the night__ is

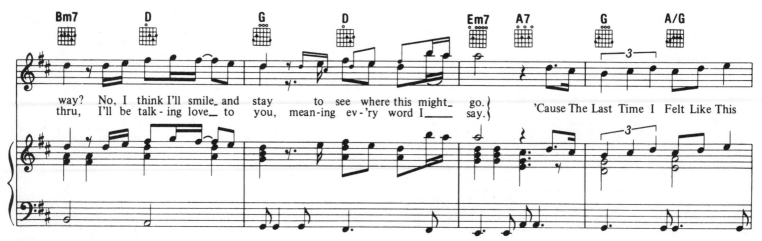

way? No, I think I'll smile__ and stay to see where this might__ go.
thru, I'll be talk - ing love__ to you, mean-ing ev-'ry word I____ say. } 'Cause The Last Time I Felt Like This

LET IT BE ME
(JE T'APPARTIENS)

English Words by MANN CURTIS
French Words by PIERRE DELANOE
Music by GILBERT BECAUD

Relaxed

I bless the day I found you, I want to stay a-round you,
If, for each bit of glad-ness, Some-one must taste of sad-ness,

And so I beg you, let it be me. Don't take this
I'll bear the sor-row, let it be me. No mat-ter

heav-en from one, If you must cling to some-one, Now and for-ev-er,
what the price is, I'll make the sac-ri-fic-es, Through each to-mor-row,

LET ME CALL YOU SWEETHEART

(I'm In Love With You)

Words by BETH SLATER WHITSON
Music by LEO FRIEDMAN

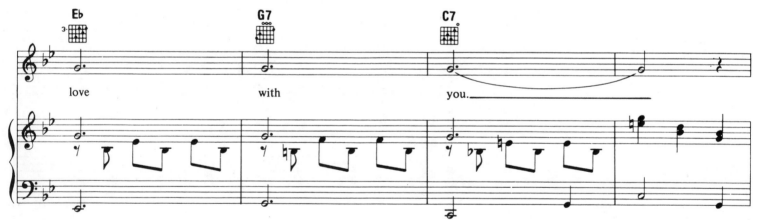

LOST IN YOUR EYES

Words and Music by
DEBORAH GIBSON

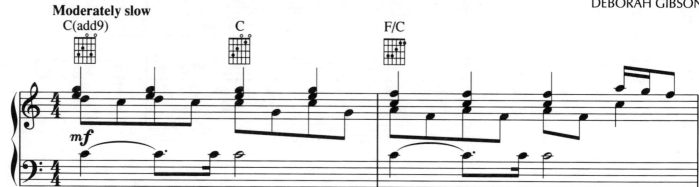

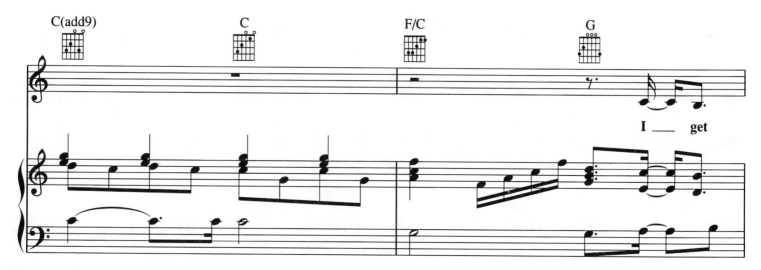

LOVE IS HERE TO STAY

(From GOLDWYN FOLLIES)

Words by IRA GERSHWIN
Music by GEORGE GERSHWIN

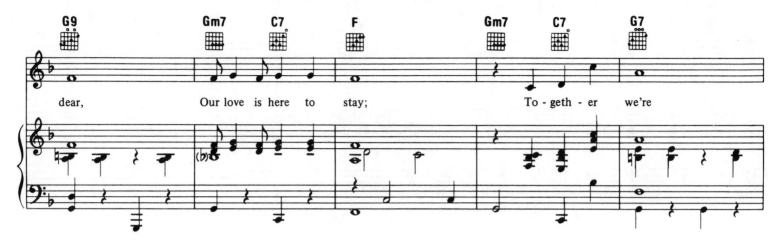

dear,   Our love is here to stay;   To - geth - er we're

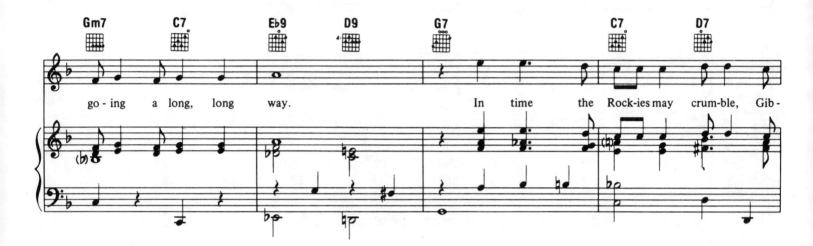

go - ing a long, long way.   In time the Rock-ies may crum-ble, Gib-

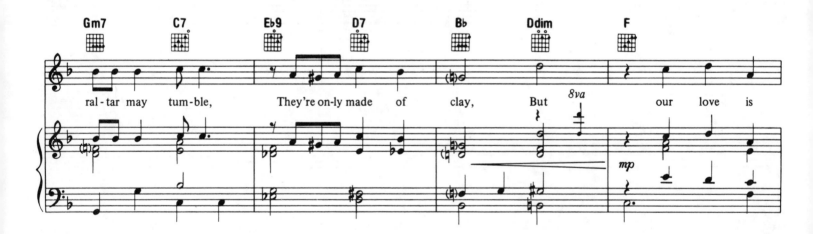

ral - tar may tum-ble,   They're on-ly made of clay,   But   our love is

here to stay.   It's ver - y   stay.

A LOVE SONG

Words and Music by
LEE GREENWOOD

MCA music publishing

LOVE ME TENDER

Words and Music by
ELVIS PRESLEY & VERA MATSON

Moderately slow

Verse

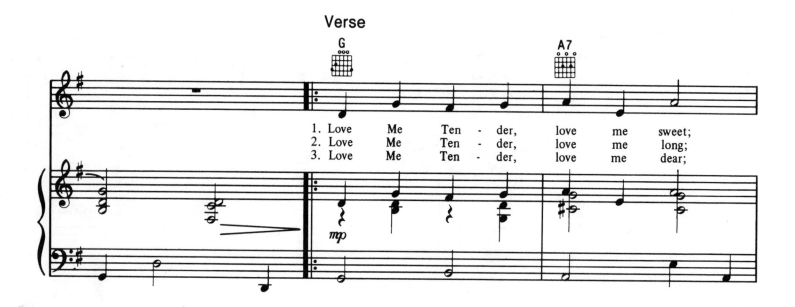

1. Love Me Ten - der, love me sweet;
2. Love Me Ten - der, love me long;
3. Love Me Ten - der, love me dear;

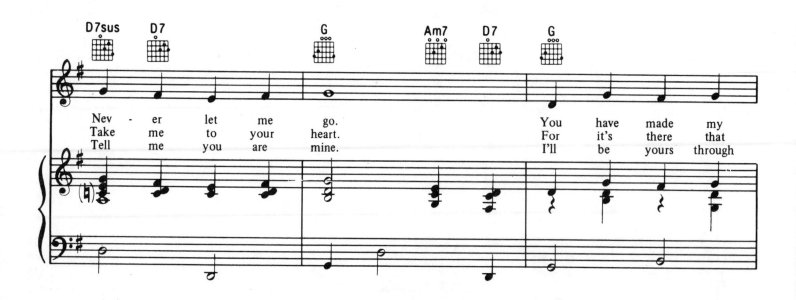

Nev - er let me go.
Take me to your heart.
Tell me you are mine.

You have made my
For it's there that
I'll be yours through

EXTRA VERSE   4. When at last my dreams come true,
                  Darling, this I know:
                  Happiness will follow you
                  Everywhere you go.

LOVE TAKES TIME

Words and Music by MARIAH CAREY
and BEN MARGULIES

LOVING YOU

Words and Music by
MIKE STOLLER and JERRY LEIBER

Moderately Slow

I will spend my whole life through Lov - ing You, ___ Lov - ing You. ___

Win - ter, sum - mer spring - time, too, Lov - ing You, ___ Lov - ing You ___

Makes no dif - f'rence where I go or what I do.

MAY YOU ALWAYS

Words and Music by LARRY MARKES
and DICK CHARLES

1. May you al - ways walk in sun - shine, slum - ber warm when
2. May good for - tune find your door - way, may the blue - bird
3. May you al - ways be a dream - er, may your wild - est

night winds blow. May you al - ways live with laugh - ter
sing your song. May no trou - ble trav - el your way,
dream come true. May you find some -

MISTY

Words by JOHNNY BURKE
Music by ERROLL GARNER

Look at me, I'm as help-less as a kit-ten up a tree And I feel like I'm cling-ing to a cloud, I can't__ un-der-stand,__ I get mist-y just hold-ing your hand._____ Walk my way and a

MORE
(Theme From MONDO CANE)

English Words by NORMAN NEWELL
Music by RIZ ORTOLANI and NINO OLIVIERO

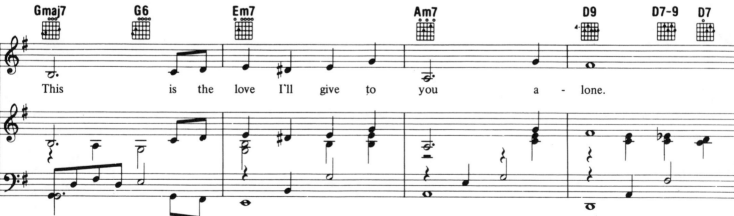

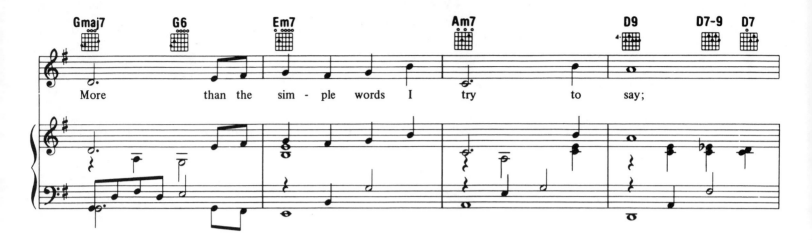

More than the sim - ple words I try to say;

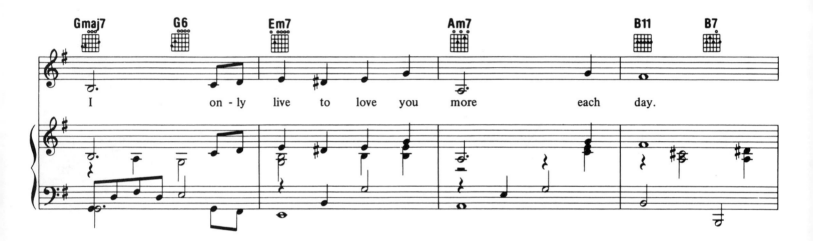

I on - ly live to love you more each day.

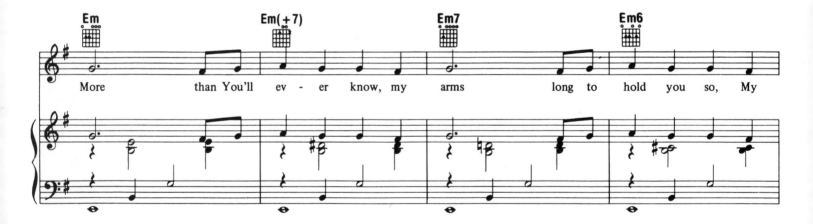

More than You'll ev - er know, my arms long to hold you so, My

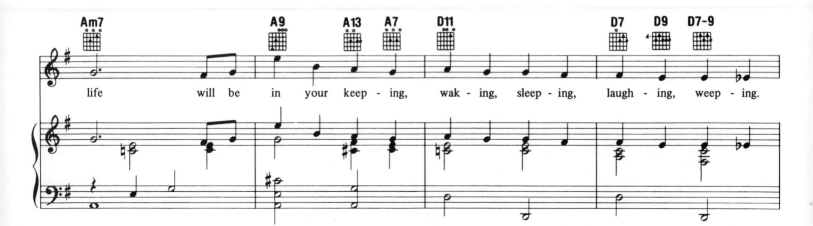

life will be in your keep - ing, wak - ing, sleep - ing, laugh - ing, weep - ing.

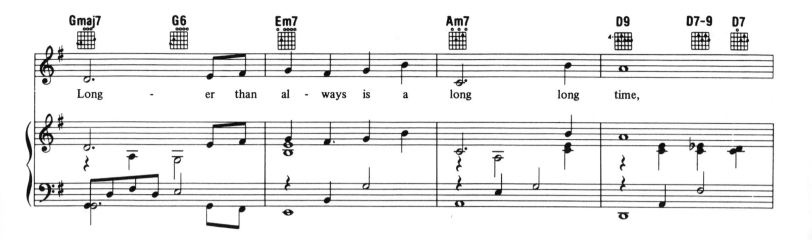

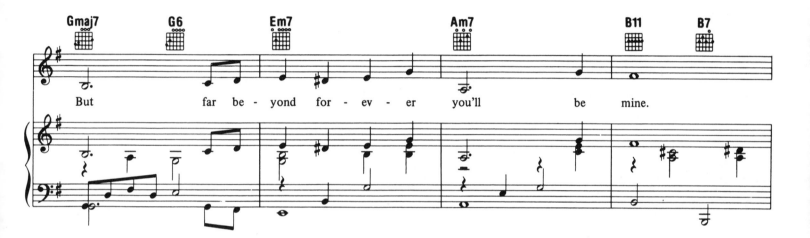

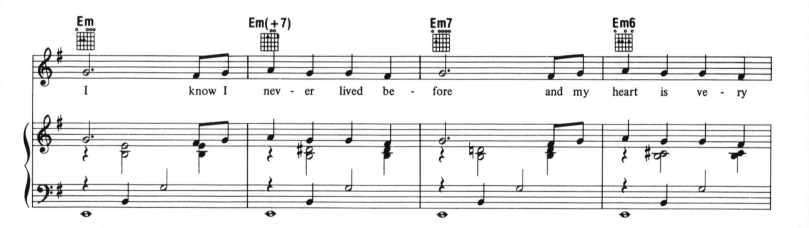

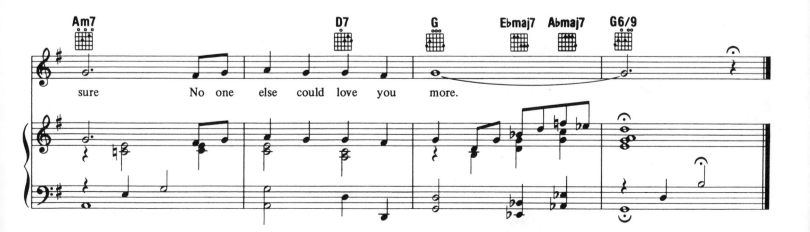

MY CUP RUNNETH OVER
(From "I DO! I DO!")

Words by TOM JONES
Music by HARVEY SCHMIDT

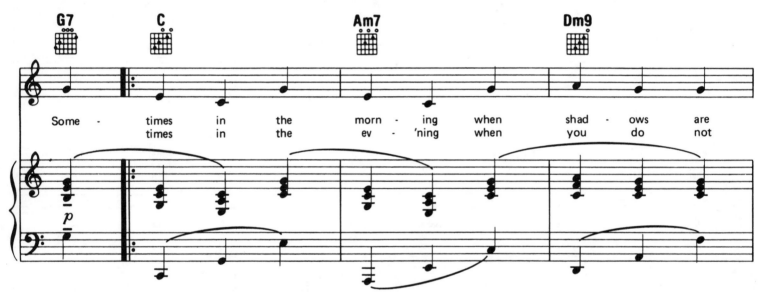

Some - times in the morn - ing when shad - ows are
times in the ev - 'ning when when you do not

deep, I lie here be - side you, just watch - ing you
see, I stud - y the small things just you do con - stant -

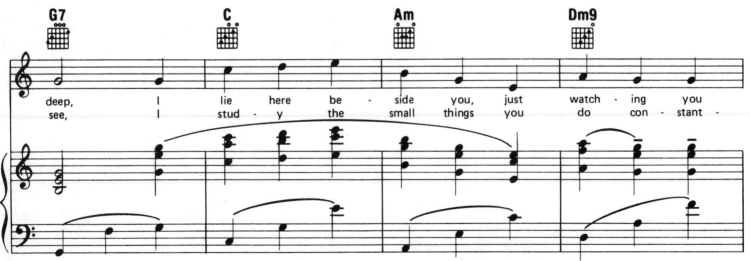

MY FUNNY VALENTINE
(From "BABES IN ARMS")

Words by LORENZ HART
Music by RICHARD RODGERS

P.S. I LOVE YOU

Words by JOHNNY MERCER
Music by GORDON JENKINS

SEA OF LOVE

Words and Music by GEORGE KHOURY
and PHILIP BASTISTE

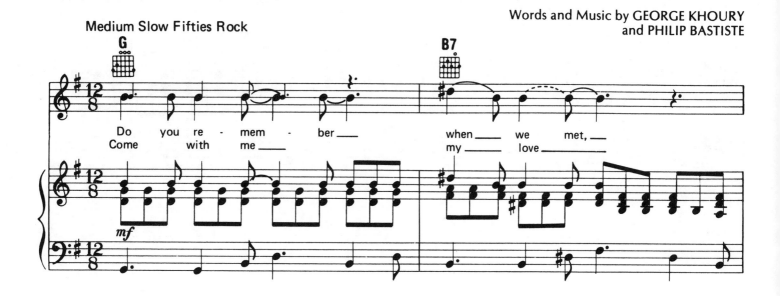

Do you re-mem-ber __ when __ we met, __
Come with me __ my __ love __

that's the day __ I knew you were my pet.
to the sea, __ the sea __ of love. __
I __ want to tell you

(just) how __ much __ I love you __

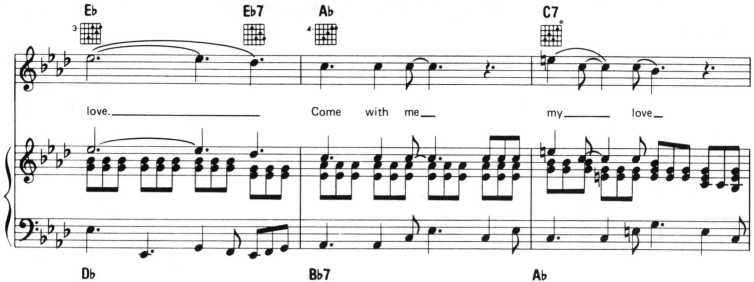

love._____ Come with me___ my_____ love_

to the sea,_____ the sea___ of love.___ I___ want to tell you

just how__ much I love you.__

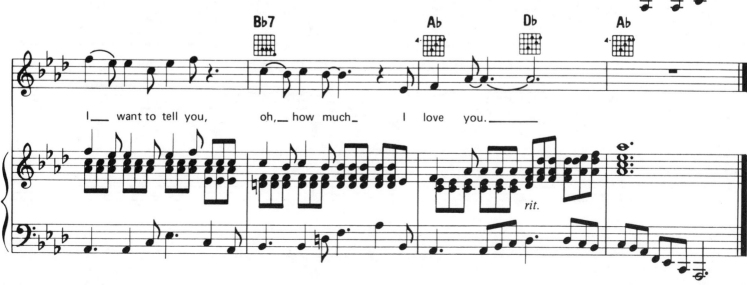

I___ want to tell you, oh,__ how much_ I love you._____

rit.

SEPTEMBER MORN

Words and Music by NEIL DIAMOND
and GILBERT BECAUD

Moderately slow

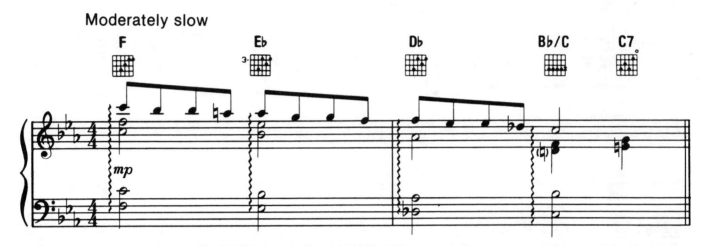

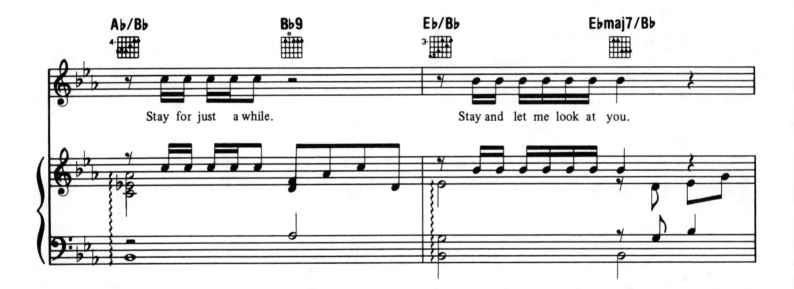

Stay for just a while. Stay and let me look at you.

It's been so long, I hard-ly knew you standing in the door.

a tempo

SHARE YOUR LOVE WITH ME

Words and Music by DEADRICK MALONE
and AL BRAGGS

Moderately slow

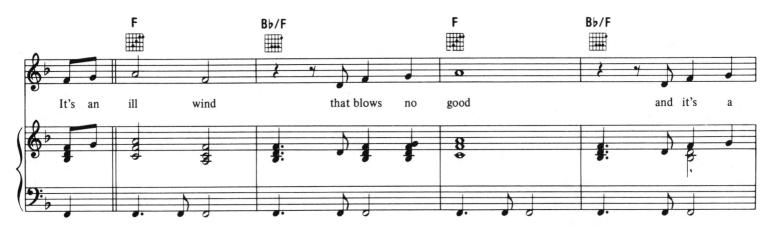

It's an ill wind that blows no good and it's a

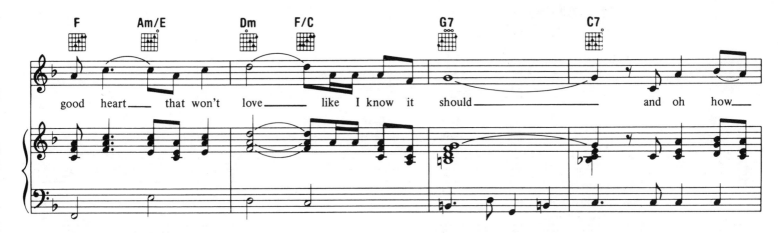

good heart___ that won't love___ like I know it should_____ and oh how___

lone-some_____ I know you must be and it's a shame___ if you don't

MCA music publishing

SHE BELIEVES IN ME

Slowly with movement

Words & Music by STEVE GIBB

SO IN LOVE

(From "KISS ME KATE")

Words and Music by COLE PORTER

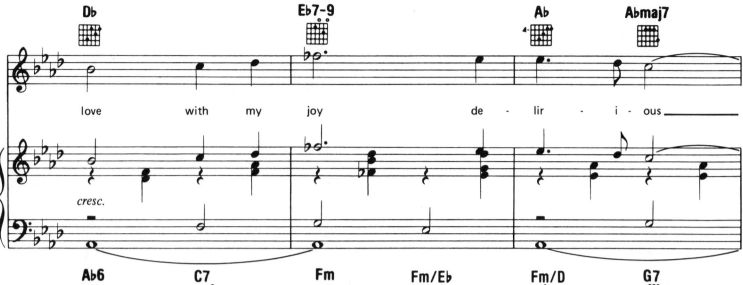

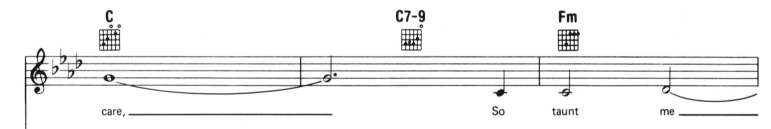

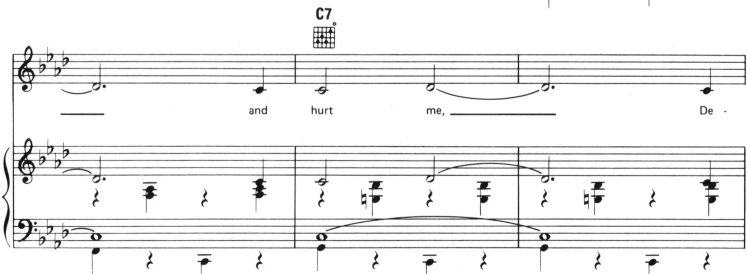

love   with   you,   my   love _____   am

SOME ENCHANTED EVENING
(From "SOUTH PACIFIC")

Words by OSCAR HAMMERSTEIN II
Music by RICHARD RODGERS

SOMETHING

Words and Music by
GEORGE HARRISON

Some-thing in____ the way____ she moves,____
Some-where in____ her smile____ she knows,____
Some-thing in____ the way____ she knows,____

at - tracts____ me like____ no oth-er lov - er.
that I____ don't need____ no oth-er lov - er.
and all____ I have__ to do is think__ of her.

Some-thing in____ the way____ she woos_____ me.____
Some-thing in____ her style____ that shows_____ me.____
Some-thing in____ the things__ she shows_____ me.____

I don't want to leave__ her now,   you

SUNRISE, SUNSET
(From the Musical "FIDDLER ON THE ROOF")

Words by SHELDON HARNICK
Music by JERRY BOCK

Moderately Slow Waltz Tempo
(soulful and wistful)

Is this the lit-tle boy I car - ried? Is this the lit-tle girl at
Now is the lit-tle boy a bride - groom, Now is the lit-tle girl a

play? I don't re - mem-ber grow-ing old - er,
bride. Un - der the can-o-py I see them,

When did they? When did she get to be a
Side by side. Place the gold ring a - round her

TILL

Words by CARL SIGMAN
Music by CHARLES DANVERS

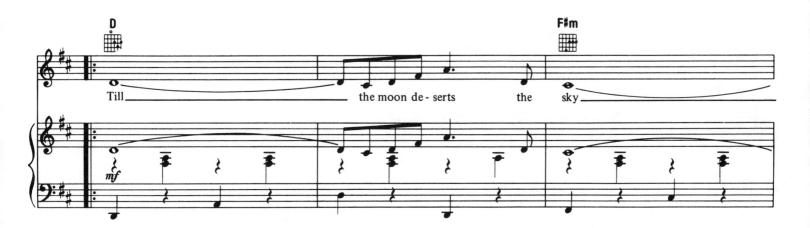

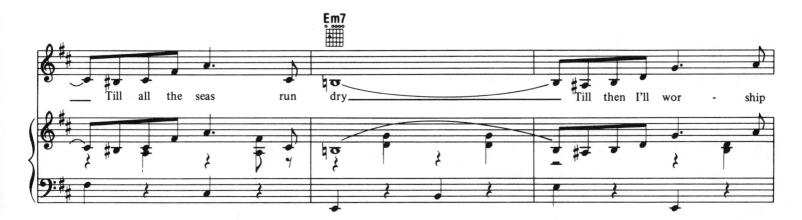

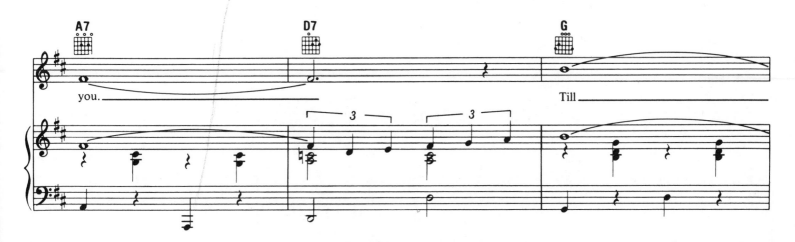

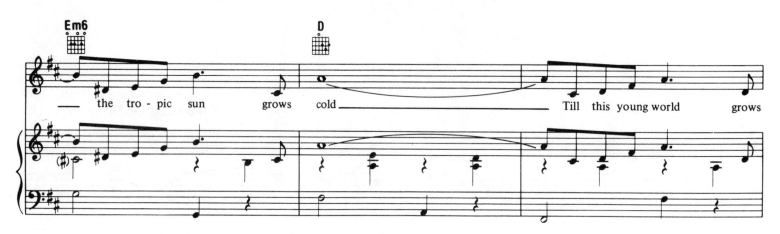

the tro - pic sun grows cold _____ Till this young world grows

old _____ My dar - ling I'll a - dore

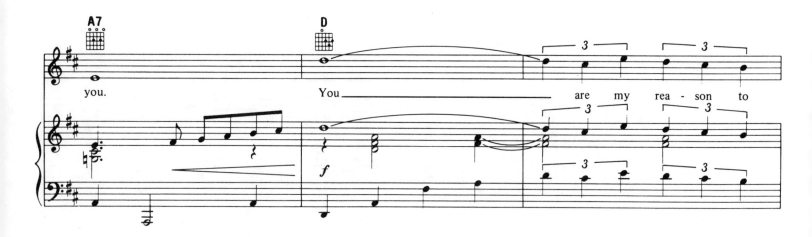

you. You _____ are my rea - son to

live _____ All I own I would give _____

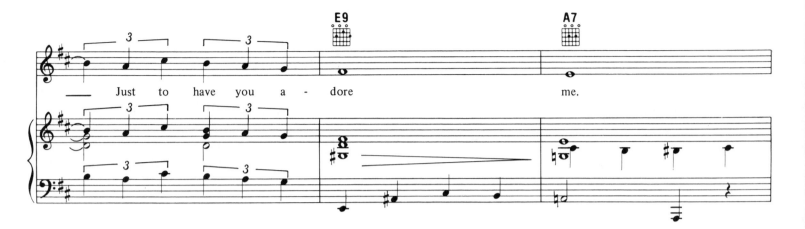

Just to have you a - dore me.

Till the riv-ers flow up-stream

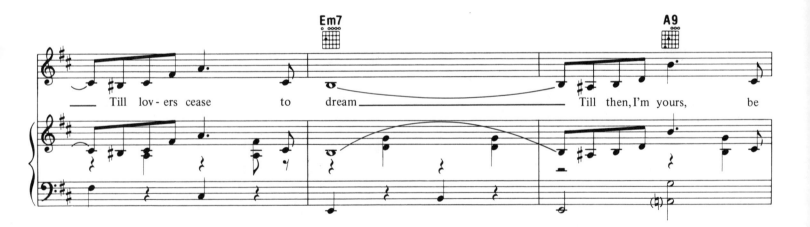

Till lov-ers cease to dream. Till then, I'm yours, be

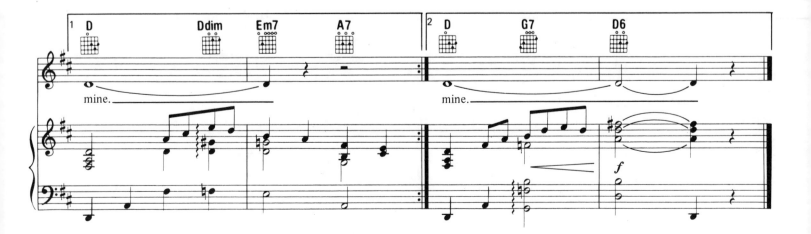

mine. mine.

THROUGH THE YEARS

Words and Music by
STEVE DORFF and MARTY PANZER

Appreciatively

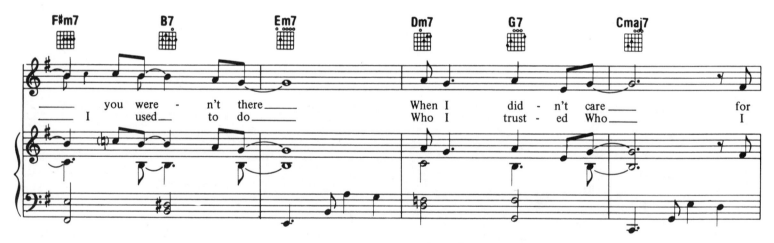

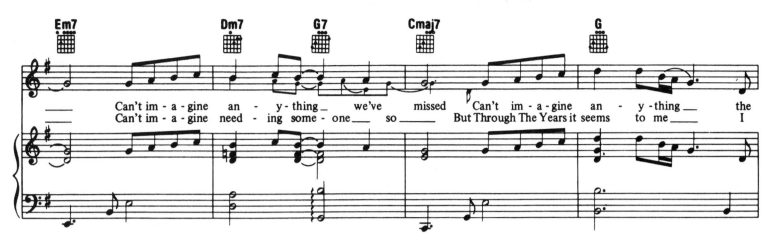

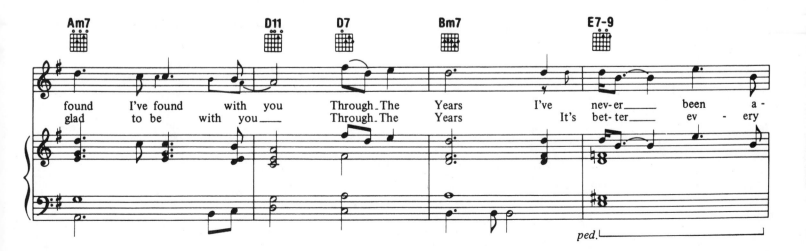

TO LOVE AGAIN
(Theme From "The Eddy Duchin Story")
Based on Chopin's E flat Nocturne

Words by NED WASHINGTON
Music by MORRIS STOLOFF & GEORGE SIDNEY

Moderately

No

heart _____ should re- fuse love, How luck - y are the

ones who choose love And if we should

lose love We have the right To Love Aa little faster

gain. _____ In a world full of

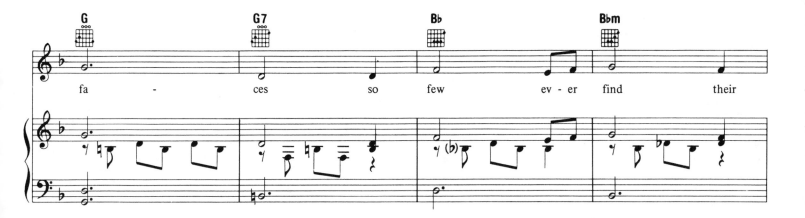

fa - ces so few ev - er find their

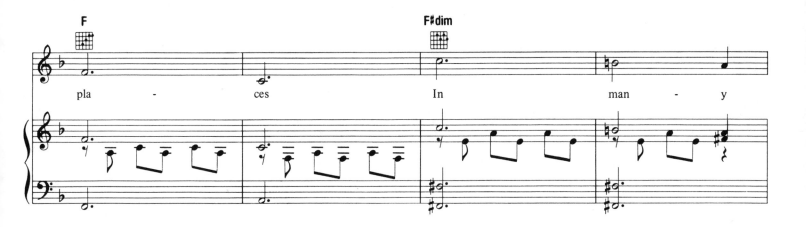

pla - ces In man - y

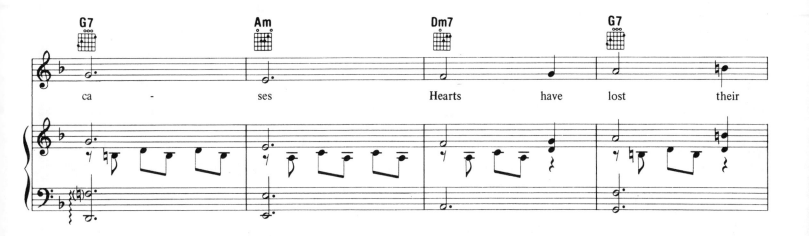

ca - ses Hearts have lost their

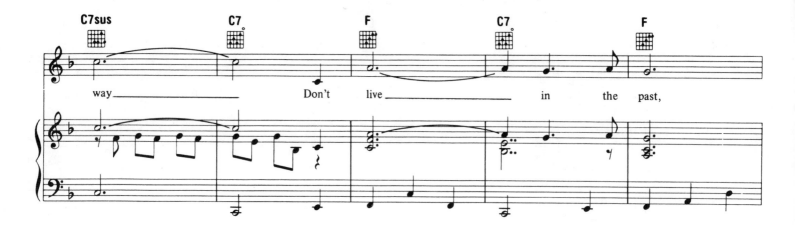

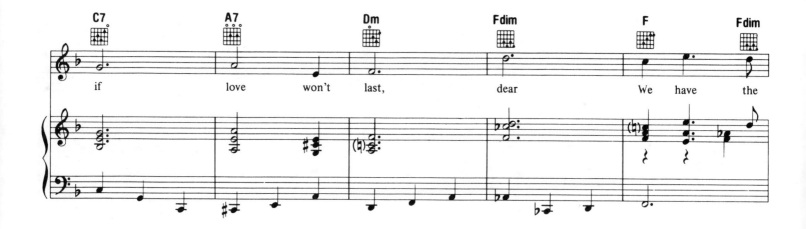

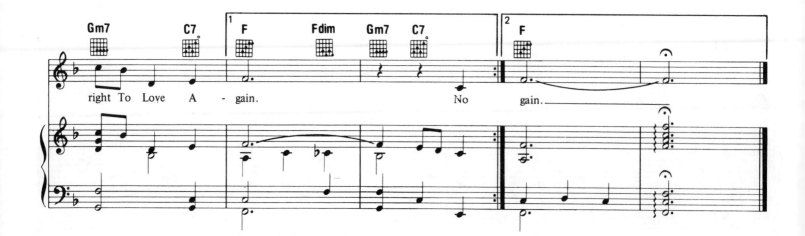

VISION OF LOVE

Words and Music by MARIAH CAREY
and BEN MARGULIES

TRUE LOVE

Words and Music by
COLE PORTER

Moderately Slow

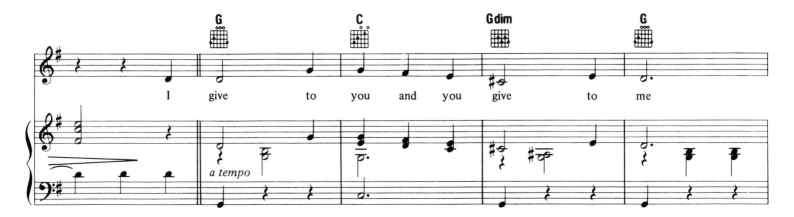

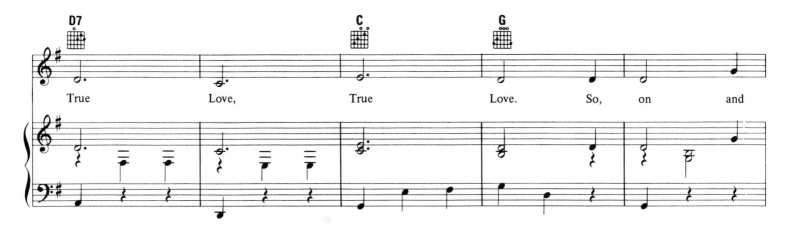

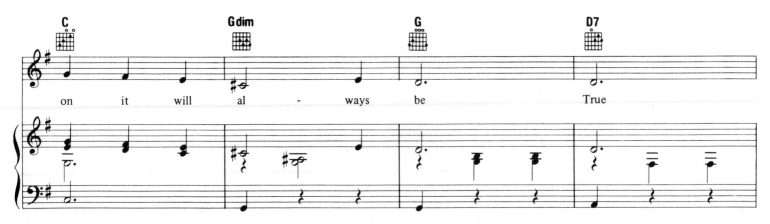

TRY TO REMEMBER

(From "THE FANTASTICKS")

Words by TOM JONES
Music by HARVEY SCHMIDT

Slowly, with tenderness

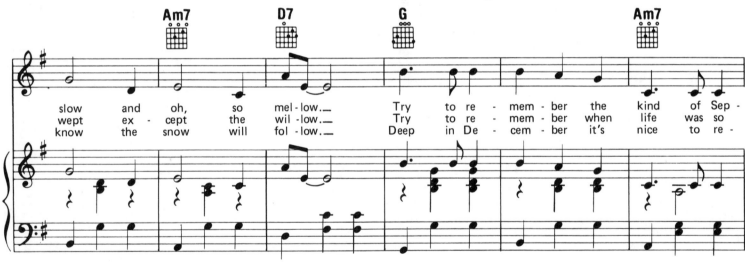

Try to re-mem-ber the kind of Sep-tem-ber when life was
Try to re-mem-ber when life was so ten-der that no one
Deep in De-cem-ber it's nice to re-mem-ber al-tho' you

slow and oh, so mel-low.__ Try to re-mem-ber the kind of Sep-
wept ex-cept so the wil-low.__ Try to re-mem-ber when life was so
know the snow will fol-low.__ Deep in De-cem-ber it's nice to re-

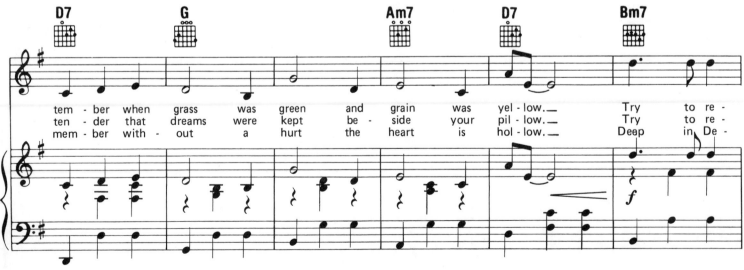

tem-ber when grass was green and grain was yel-low.__ Try to re-
ten-der that dreams were kept be-side your pil-low.__ Try to re-
mem-ber with-out a hurt the heart is hol-low.__ Deep in De-

WHAT THE WORLD NEEDS NOW IS LOVE

Lyric by HAL DAVID
Music by BURT BACHARACH

WHEN I FALL IN LOVE

Words by EDWARD HEYMAN
Music by VICTOR YOUNG

WHEN I NEED YOU

Words by CAROLE BAYER SAGER
Music by ALBERT HAMMOND

Moderately, with feeling

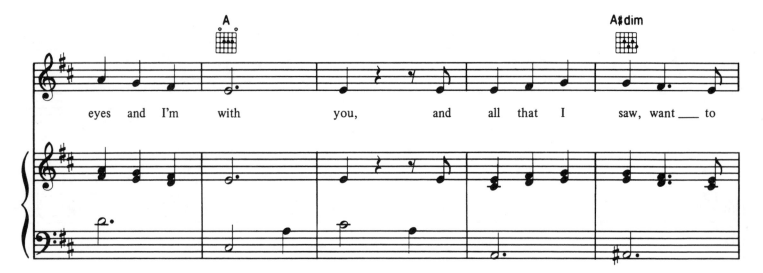

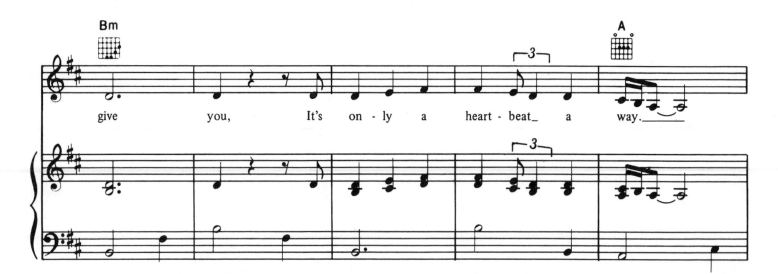

A tel - e-phone can't take the place of your smile.___
Hon-ey, that's a heav - y load that we bear.___

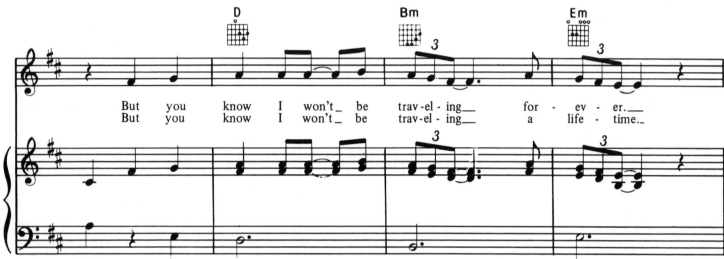

But you know I won't_ be trav-el-ing___ for - ev - er.___
But you know I won't_ be trav-el-ing___ a life - time..

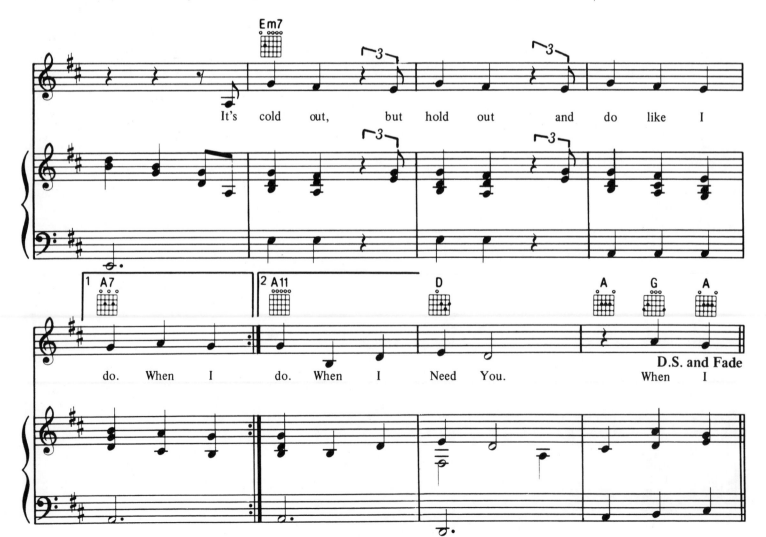

It's cold out, but hold out and do like I

do. When I do. When I Need You.

D.S. and Fade

When I

WOMAN

Words and Music by
JOHN LENNON

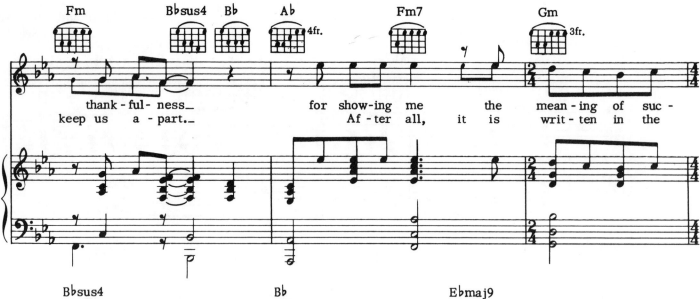

thank-ful-ness___ for show-ing me the mean-ing of suc-
keep us a-part.___ Af-ter all, it is writ-ten in the

cess. _____
stars. _____

Ooh, _____

well, well. Doo doo doo doo doo. Ooh, _____

well, well. Doo doo doo doo doo. doo doo.

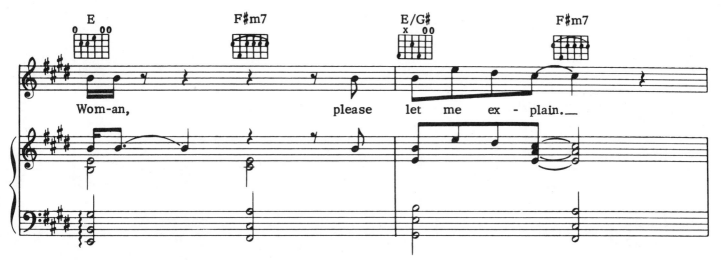

Wom-an, please let me ex - plain.__

I nev-er meant to cause you sor-row or pain.__ So let me tell you a-

gain and a - gain and a - gain:_____ I

Repeat and fade

love _____ you, yeah, yeah, now and for - ev-er. I

WOMAN IN LOVE

Words and Music by
BARRY GIBB and ROBIN GIBB

Moderately Slow

Life is a mo-ment in space,___ when the dream is gone___ it's a lone-li-er place.___
With you e-ter-nal-ly mine,___ in love there is___ no meas-ure of time.___

YOU ARE MY LADY

Words and Music by
BARRY J. EASTMOND

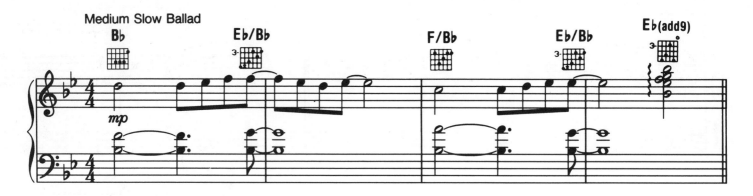

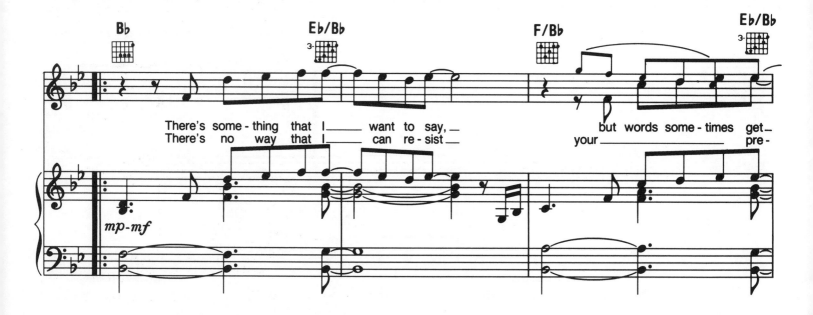

YOU GIVE GOOD LOVE

Words and Music by
LAFORREST "LA LA" COPE

Verse 1:

1. I found out what I've been miss - ing, al - ways on the run.

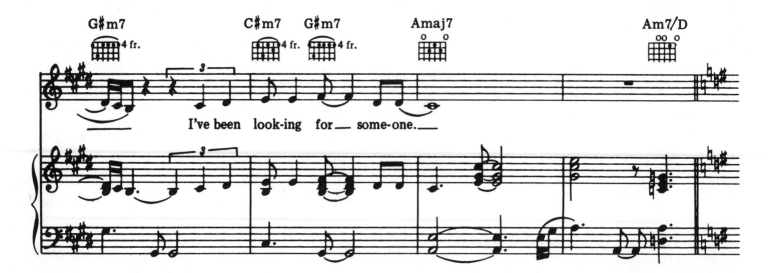

I've been look-ing for some-one.

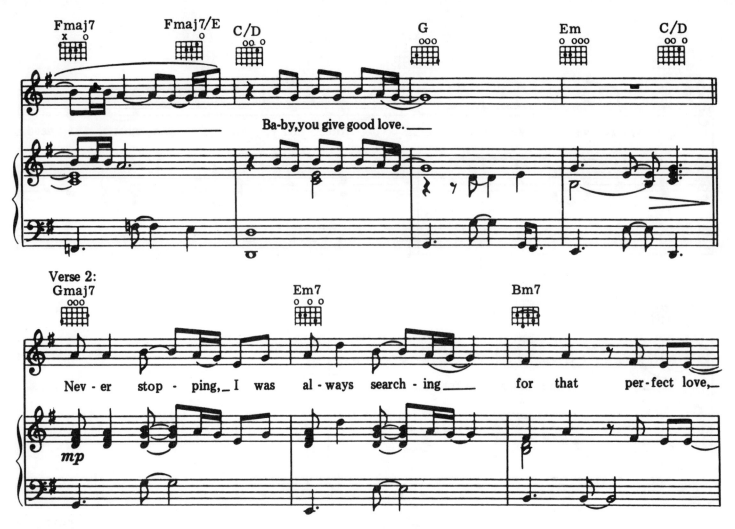

Ba-by, you give good love. ____

Verse 2:

Nev-er stop-ping,_ I was al-ways search-ing ____ for that per-fect love,

the kind that girls like me__ dream of. ____

Now you're here__ like you've been ____ be-fore,__ and you know__ just what__ I need.__

YOU NEEDED ME

Words and Music by RANDY GOODRUM

Moderately

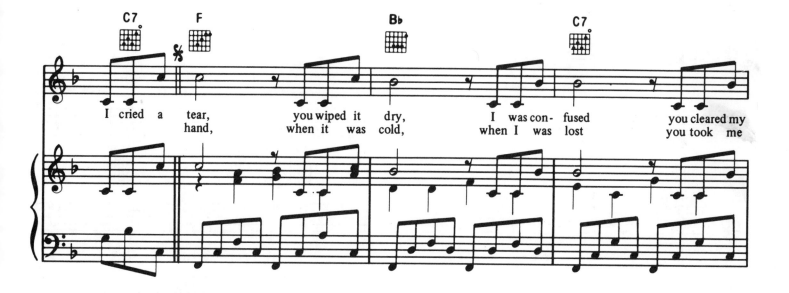

I cried a tear, you wiped it dry, I was con- fused you cleared my
hand, when it was cold, when I was lost you took me

mind, I sold my soul, you bought it back for me__ and held me
home You gave me hope, when I was at the end__ and turned my

YOUR SONG

Slow, but with a beat

Words and Music by ELTON JOHN and BERNIE TAUPIN

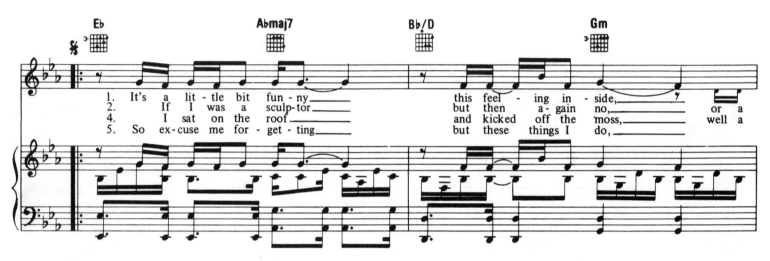

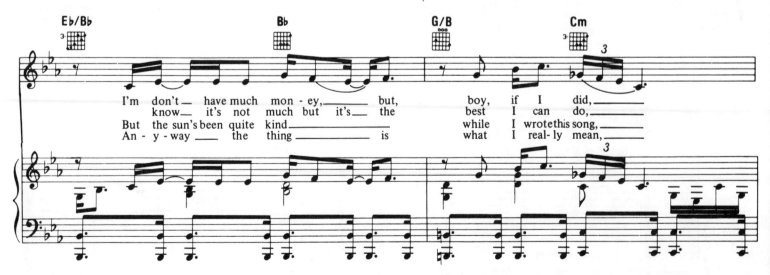

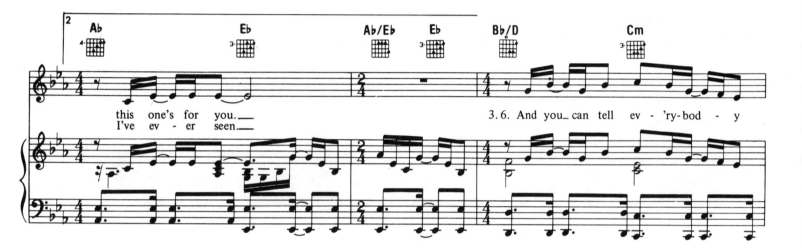

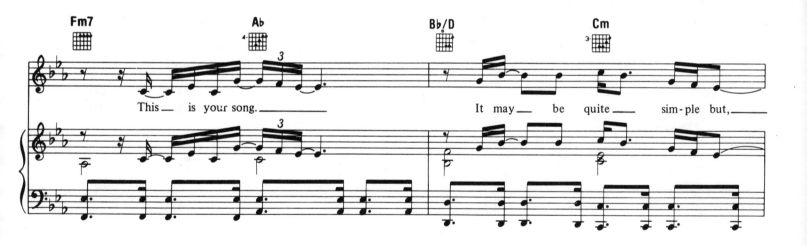